WE OUGHTA KNOW

WE OUGHTA KNOW

HOW CÉLINE, SHANIA, ALANIS, AND SARAH RULED THE '90S AND CHANGED MUSIC

ANDREA WARNER

FOREWORD BY VIVEK SHRAYA

First published in 2015 by Eternal Cavalier Press.
Expanded, updated, revised, and retitled for 2024
via ECW Press.

Published by ECW Press
665 Gerrard Street East
Toronto, Ontario, Canada M4M 1Y2
416-694-3348 / info@ecwpress.com

Editor for the Press: Jen Sookfong Lee
Copy editor: Jen Knoch
Cover design: Michel Vrana

LIBRARY AND ARCHIVES CANADA CATALOGUING IN PUBLICATION

Title: We oughta know : how Céline, Shania, Alanis, and Sarah ruled the '90s and changed music / Andrea Warner ; foreword by Vivek Shraya.

Names: Warner, Andrea, author. | Shraya, Vivek, 1981- author of introduction, etc.

Identifiers: Canadiana (print) 20240372581 | Canadiana (ebook) 20240372603

ISBN 978-1-77041-774-8 (softcover)
ISBN 978-1-77852-328-1 (ePub)
ISBN 978-1-77852-329-8 (PDF)

Subjects: LCSH: Women singers—Canada—History and criticism. | LCSH: Popular music—Canada—1991-2000. | LCSH: Music, Influence of.

Classification: LCC ML3484 .W279 2024 | DDC 782.421640971—dc23

This book is funded in part by the Government of Canada. Ce livre est financé en partie par le gouvernement du Canada. We acknowledge the support of the Canada Council for the Arts. Nous remercions le Conseil des arts du Canada de son soutien. We would like to acknowledge the funding support of the Ontario Arts Council (OAC) and the Government of Ontario for their support. We also acknowledge the support of the Government of Ontario through the Ontario Book Publishing Tax Credit, and through Ontario Creates.

Canada Council for the Arts
Conseil des arts du Canada

ONTARIO ARTS COUNCIL
CONSEIL DES ARTS DE L'ONTARIO
an Ontario government agency
un organisme du gouvernement de l'Ontario

PRINTED AND BOUND IN CANADA

PRINTING: FRIESENS 5 4 3 2 1

This book is dedicated to everybody who is starting to understand and confront the mess of their own internalized misogyny. Solidarity and love to all of us works-in-progress.

CONTENTS

FOREWORD

The (White) Woman in Me by Vivek Shraya

I attended my very first concert in the summer of 1996 at the Edmonton Coliseum. The opening acts were Frente! and Our Lady Peace, but I was there for the headliner: Alanis Morissette. I don't remember the night's intricate details (aside from somehow sleeping through OLP's raucous set—sorry, Raine!), likely because I was fifteen years old and my $20-a-week allowance could only buy me tickets high up in the rafters. What I do remember is Alanis's *voice*, the way it defiantly reverberated throughout the arena.

Like millions of teenagers (and moms) in the '90s, I knew every word of *Jagged Little Pill*. I would argue that many of us were initially lured by Alanis's lyrics: her unexpected word choices (hello, "intellectual intercourse" and "back-loaded puppet"), her odd yet somehow catchy phrasing (I spent many, many years singing "cross-eyed bear"), and, of course, the unfiltered explorations of sex, abuse of power, and rejection. So it's easy to overlook the fact that Alanis has a stunning, expansive vocal range and capacity. But it couldn't be overlooked that night at the Coliseum.

Even before I was officially a singer, it had always been voices that drew me to music. I'm fascinated by how much a voice can do technically and convey emotionally, how far it can reach beyond the body and burrow itself in someone else's body and memory. This is the main reason I always attribute my induction into Western pop music to Whitney Houston (a.k.a. the greatest voice of all time) and other Black female vocalists like Mariah and Brandy, and to '90s R&B broadly, where so much emphasis was on melody, riffs, and belting.

In the mid-'90s, my tastes started to widen to a "genre" that featured Alanis, Sheryl Crow, and Tori Amos, a genre that a popular compilation of the time attempted to blanket classify as "Women & Songs." Once again, I was captivated by these women's distinctive voices: PJ Harvey's snarl, Fiona Apple's bass, and Sarah McLachlan's breathtaking falsetto.

As a child, I was prone to singing in a high register (we can thank my parents' Bollywood soundtracks for this), but by mid-puberty, my voice was changing. I worried about losing those precious high notes, but even puberty could not stop me from squeaking along with McLachlan's otherworldly falsetto track "Fear" — which my best friend and I would crank in his candlelit basement, trying to communicate with the spirit world. (FYI, the cult classic film *The Craft* and *Fumbling Towards Ecstasy* are soul sisters.)

Obsessively reading Andrea Warner's multifaceted *We Oughta Know* years later instantly brought me back to that time of first concerts and midnight seances. The book creates a compelling snapshot of what it meant to grow up in Canada in the '90s, surrounded at all times by Alanis Morissette, Sarah McLachlan, Céline Dion, and Shania Twain — very different artists who somehow built our collective coming-of-age soundtrack. Living in Canada, however, also meant that I didn't quite grasp the magnitude of these women's careers and successes, so it was also mind-blowing reading Warner elaborate on their *global* impact. Bigger than the Beatles — what?

We Oughta Know has also undoubtedly been on the forefront of the recent surge of films about and by women artists. These docs and biopics have allowed us to hear directly from artists — including Alanis and Shania — about the relentless sexism and misogyny that they endured. But all too often, many of these films end up focusing more on the controversies (read: men) that surrounded (read: hurt) the artist — Tina Turner's horrific experiences of domestic violence, the fallout after Sinéad O'Connor ripped up the photo of the Pope, and Janet Jackson's family dynamics — and less on their beloved art. Can you imagine a Beck or Lenny Kravitz documentary that centred their love lives instead of rare studio footage or interviews about cool guitar sounds? *We Oughta Know* is so special, in part, because of the pages and pages Warner devotes to the actual music, the albums, *the songs* (even the ones she doesn't like!) made by its groundbreaking subjects. Alanis, Sarah, Céline, and Shania deserve nothing less.

Revisiting *We Oughta Know* in this rigorous new edition, I found myself relating (albeit differently) to Warner's poignant personal disclosures about how pivotal these artists were in shaping her girlhood and feminism, particularly her complicated reckoning with Céline and Shania. Like Warner, I, too, felt less of a connection to these artists growing up. Or so I thought.

I started to recall when Céline's "The Power of Love" music video was on heavy rotation on MuchMusic. Her bedroom sensuality, coupled with the chorus lyrics, made me feel like *I* was someone's lady. Or rather made me want to know what it would feel like to be someone's lady. Similarly, I also remember accidentally landing on the video for Shania's "The Woman in Me" on Country Music Television while flipping between my soaps, being transfixed by the image of Shania crooning through her windswept white sheet, and having similar feelings of longing for a man in my heart.

As Warner points out, wanting to "belong" to a man is not very feminist, at least in the traditional sense. But as a closeted queer teenaged boy who would come out as trans decades later, these two songs allowed me to own the words "lady" and "woman" — as I belted along in the safety of my bedroom — while also expressing my desire for men. And so, I'm grateful to Céline and Shania for their voices, too, and the impact they had on mine.

The final concert I attended in the '90s also happened to be the last ever Lilith Fair concert (lucky Edmonton). My best friend and I stood for hours in the rain, pushed against the metal barricades at the front, and soaked in the music of Sarah McLachlan, Sheryl Crow, the Chicks, Indigo Girls, and Deborah Cox. It was a glorious night and fitting end to a tremendous, turbulent musical decade.

In the 2000s, cassettes, CDs, and essentially *music* as a physical art commodity would tragically disappear. Perhaps not coincidentally, so much of the music history and contributions made in the '90s (and earlier), especially those by marginalized artists, are still undocumented and not fairly lauded. And as Warner notes, very little has changed when examining gender equity in the music industry. But I still take comfort in the small nods to the lasting impact of female artists of the '90s — like the annual Spotify Wrapped playlist featuring a genre called "Lilith." And big ones, like this comprehensive, engrossing book you are holding in your hands.

INTRODUCTION

One of my favourite pieces of musical trivia is this: in Canada, up until 2015 at least, Céline Dion was bigger than the Beatles. So were Alanis Morissette, Shania Twain, and Sarah McLachlan. In fact, according to the 2010 Nielsen SoundScan, of the ten best-selling artists in Canada, only five were Canadian and all five were women. Céline Dion was first, then Morissette and Twain, with McLachlan in sixth. Diana Krall was tenth. The Beatles made an underwhelming appearance at number seven.

This chart still reflects a couple of major truths: there were only five Canadians on the list of best-selling artists in Canada. The top four — Dion, Morissette, Twain, and McLachlan — all burst into prominence during a five-year window from 1993 to 1997. Suddenly an impressive statistic becomes a *holy shit* one. How did these four wildly different artists have such a chokehold on the charts and the culture that they not only changed the gender dynamics of the music industry but also changed music itself?

Yes, of course, the '90s were a different time. Much to the chagrin of audio purists, people began to embrace CDs over vinyl records and cassette tapes. It was a glorious transition for the ashen-eared non-audiophiles, even while purists resisted, eventually resurrecting vinyl and cassettes. The decade was the final heyday of physical record sales before the bottom fell out in the aughts with file sharing and streaming. But even considering the music industry's drastic changes, would the average person ever have guessed that four women — *Canadian* women — were among the best-selling artists in Canada? For example, when critics talked about famous, mainstream Canadian musicians and acts in 2010, masculine acts like Nickelback, Drake, and Michael Bublé typically got priority. Almost fifteen years later, it's now the Weeknd, Justin Bieber, and, well, Drake is still holding on. It's a fascinating, exciting, inspiring thing to think that amidst all the bullshit sexism — in the music industry and in the world — these women defied the odds, their critics, and the general consensus that rock 'n' roll is a man's space to succeed. Consider that as recently as 2023, *Rolling Stone* magazine founder Jann Wenner went on the record with the *New York Times* and declared that his new book, *The Masters*, did not include any women or Black artists because they "didn't articulate" at the "intellectual level" of their white male peers.[1]

So. Many. Questions. About Wenner's racist, sexist nonsense, and also about how, in the face of prevailing, gate-keeping attitudes like his, Dion, Twain, Morissette, and McLachlan became the big four in Canadian music? What's the Venn diagram shared by a grande dame of ballads, a country-pop queen, a hissing alt-rock viper, and an angelic folkie? Is Canada a secret feminist

---

1 David Marchese, "Jann Wenner Defends His Legacy, and His Generation's," *New York Times*, September 15, 2023, https://www.nytimes.com/2023/09/15/arts/jann-wenner-the-masters-interview.html.

wonderland or a hothouse of terrible taste where emotions are easily, voluntarily manipulated? What was it about 1993 to 1997, *my* prime teenage years (fourteen to eighteen years old), that made it possible for this particular confluence of events? I hated Dion and Twain when I was a teenager. The cheesy sincerity, skimpy outfits, and simpering "love is everything" mantras were an affront to the sarcastic, smarty, arty persona I was trying to cultivate. How the hell did I get to the point where I wanted to write a book that included them and their perky, earnest superstardom? I was team Morissette and McLachlan forever; how did I get so soft? How did we get here?

It's as if Canada took the essence of the Riot Grrrl movement — made famous in the early '90s by unrepentant feminist bands like Bratmobile, Bikini Kill, and 7 Year Bitch — and put it through some kind of sanitized metamorphosis. Riot Grrrl's third-wave radical feminism was political, punk, and DIY. The prominence of Dion, Twain, Morissette, and McLachlan was like a triple distillation — cannibalization, commodification, and gentrification — of Riot Grrrl's ethos applied across four totally different genres of music. Their success wasn't antithetical exactly, but it illustrated the spectrum of influence women were having across music in the '90s and how the razor-sharp edge of the Riot Grrrls could be softened, monetized, and sold in huge numbers. The sheer force of Dion's, Twain's, Morissette's, and McLachlan's international impact was a bizarre show of strength on Canada's part, completely unheard of and unique in terms of dominating mainstream music charts, that ultimately ushered in a new era of music in this country.

It's time to pay tribute and dig a little deeper into the hows, whys, and WTFs of those five years. In 2014, when I began writing about these four women, we had put too much distance between ourselves, their music, and the cultural context they had to navigate, leaning too heavily on scorn, ridicule, and mockery. We've started to make amends over the last decade, but there's still more work to be done.

I know from experience. I spent years giving side-eye to Dion and Twain, instead of identifying and recognizing their achievements in real time. I diminished and demeaned them without considering what that stripped from me in the process, what narratives I was reinforcing, and how I had unintentionally internalized systemic sexism and misogyny. I was a tool of the patriarchy. What a mindfuck.

All four women deserve so much more credit than they were ever given. That doesn't mean every song was great or even good, but what they did between 1993 and 1997 deserves critical examination and exploration. And not just the music, but the climate as well; there was sexism, misogyny and ageism spilling out in deliberate and casual ways from every corner of the media — from critics to DJs and VJs to music programmers — all clutching their pearls while the politics of feminism was spreading everywhere. The debate was as loud and furious then as it is now, albeit in different ways. (The broader strokes of feminism were once the focus of mainstream conversation whereas now there's more interest in intersectionality, trans-inclusive feminism, and confronting the ways in which white feminists uphold white supremacy.) But for five years, Dion, Twain, Morissette, and McLachlan, four larger-than-life, hugely successful women, were everything and were driving feminist conversation, whether they ever intended to or not. It was a monumental time in Canadian pop culture, and it changed the music industry here and abroad. It also changed me.

It's been ten years since I wrote the first iteration of this book, and the '90s revival is still going strong. In part, it has manifested as an ongoing and never-ending series of exercises: identifying entrenched sexism and misogyny and unpacking how both shaped culture and taste; confronting and identifying institutional and systemic barriers as well as personal complicity and accountability; and envisioning and enacting a more inclusive and intersectional feminism. It's exhausting, and in a lot of ways, I'm angrier than I've ever been, yet my rage is more focused because I'm better equipped and empowered to name it. And the credit is due to the extraordinary folks who are coming up behind me: younger intersectional feminists who are often racialized, queer, gender fluid, and/or nonbinary, who loudly name and call out transphobia, gendered violence, racism, sexism, misogyny, homophobia, white supremacy, bullying, ableism, fatphobia, and other toxic behaviours for what they are. No euphemisms, no excuses, no tolerance for inflicting harm or wielding power in oppressive, punishing ways.

I am thrilled and fascinated by the recent desire and demand for media, moguls, fans, and haters alike to reconsider what we think we know about infamous and invisible women; to consider who has been vilified or erased or exploited and/or all of the above. The focus on the '90s isn't surprising, as it marked a turning point in media: the internet was in its infancy, the massive magazine collapse of the early to mid-2000s was on the other side of a looming Y2K panic, and "feminism" was less a shorthand for equality and empowerment and more a code that was conflated with hating men and girl power. Queen Latifah, TLC, Hole, Liz Phair, Alanis Morissette, Spice Girls, Britney Spears, Avril Lavigne — this is just a cursory overview of the women artists who continue to spark conversation about the ways in which feminism was represented, contested, and refuted in '90s music. Most were scrutinized and exploited in different ways and to different extents, whereas others were essentially ignored, erased, and discounted. Every which way, it was rarely about the music and much more about their bodies, looks, sexuality, dating history, and policing their attitudes, personalities, and choices. This current reckoning of women reclaiming their agency, telling their own stories, and correcting the skewed, sexist, misogynist, racist, ableist record has been a long time coming. It's a powerful and important counternarrative. But it doesn't make up for what women artists lived through all those years ago.

In the last decade, Twain, Dion, Morissette, and McLachlan have all found themselves back in the spotlight. Twain launched a massive comeback with 2017's *Now*, her first album of new material since 2002's *Up!*, and she was the subject of a 2022 documentary, *Not Just a Girl*. Dion's husband and long-time manager, René Angélil, died in 2016, and in 2022, she revealed she'd been diagnosed with stiff-person syndrome, a serious neurological condition. (She also finally became an actual fashion icon instead of just an aspirational one, through her work with stylist Law Roach). Morissette was the subject of a documentary as well (*Jagged*) but publicly disavowed it before its release, while also helping turn *Jagged Little Pill* into a Tony Award–winning Broadway musical and launching a massive *Jagged Little Pill* anniversary tour. McLachlan and Lilith Fair became the subjects of a sprawling *Vanity Fair* oral history. All four are taking back what was stripped from them, and I don't know if these cultural reappraisals and reassessments are necessarily meaningful to them personally, but they're vital to me and to many other fans in Canada and beyond. I also think it's crucial for their music catalogue to have a more just reassessment of the importance of their songs, for the artists facing similar scrutiny, hostility, and scorn now, and for everyone who directly confronts the ongoing damage of the patriarchy, including those of us who have internalized it and are trying to unlearn it.

I used to think that I was sixty-two percent *Jagged Little Pill* era Alanis and thirty-eight percent pre-*Surfacing* Sarah, but I have to admit that all four women carved out holes in my bones and settled into the marrow. When four women are such visible, inescapable forces in the pop culture of your youth, when you see four women shake the music industry from its male-dominated grip, when you realize that all four of them did this in their late teens to their mid-twenties — just a few years ahead of yourself in your mid-teens — their influence on you is like sunken treasure at the bottom of the ocean. It can take weeks, months, years, even decades before a true understanding of why you care so much comes, gloriously, to the surface.

OF FEMINIST HEROES, VAPID WONDERS, MADONNAS, AND WHORES

As a teenager, my hatred of Céline Dion and Shania Twain wasn't just about their music but their entire identities. Some of my friends loved them, but I was more discerning (okay, judgmental). I was ruled by the absolute conviction that's unburdened by life experience and perspective.

They were like an extreme real-world manifestation of one of my favourite children's book series, The Baby-Sitters Club, which centers on four very different thirteen-year-old girls who open a babysitting business in small-town Connecticut. Kristy is in charge, bossy and ambitious, and seems older than all the other kids. Though not a "tomboy" like Kristy, Céline Dion seemed like a total Kristy: entrepreneurial, assured, and possessing laser-like focus on getting what she wants. Like Kristy, Dion has always seemed fifty, even when she was fifteen (which doesn't take the "ick" factor out of her May-December marriage but does perhaps put it in perspective), singing on tracks about mature love and longing, and often styled as if she were attending a corporate networking event. Dion's drive, also preternaturally mature, has been intact since she was eight years old. It took Kristy until she was twelve, a relative slacker by comparison, to seize her vision.

Kristy's best friend is Mary Anne. She's shy and timid but has a secret wild heart just waiting to come out. She gets the first steady boyfriend in the group, which is a huge deal. That's Twain all the way: she baffles by projecting a dual image, two halves seemingly pitted against each other. The down-home good girl and sex kitten are constantly at odds, especially in her music videos. Consider "Any Man of Mine," where she's taking charge on horseback and driving a huge truck but still flashing her midriff with a T-shirt knotted above her belly button, or "No One Needs to Know," where Twain, clad in a casual but feminine denim button-down and white skirt, is sitting on a porch playing guitar with her band and singing about how she's secretly planning marriage, babies, and her future with her man, unbeknownst to him.

Claudia, my personal favourite, is Japanese-American and an artist who loves junk food and saying "Oh my lord," which for me at the time was *way* cool since it was a sacrilegious swear. She has edge and style but is still relatable. Claudia's traits are in line with Alanis Morissette's image circa *Jagged Little Pill*: fun but intense, an artist whose fashion reflects her eclectic nature, and whose wide range of emotions mirrored that of many teenaged girls who were just trying to find equilibrium between hormones, feelings, and life.

Stacey is the ultra-cool new girl who moved from New York but is still down to earth because she is diabetic and her parents are divorced. Sarah McLachlan was worldly but totally accessible around the time of *Fumbling Towards Ecstasy*, and every song felt devastatingly real, lived in, and pained. Stacey and Sarah didn't necessarily share a common fashion sense, but each possessed a singular look: Stacey was young, chic, and urban sophisticate while Sarah was young, chic, and urban hippie. Both Alanis and Sarah were young women who had seen some shit, and there was nothing more exhilarating than finding a place for my teenage angst in their authentic, grown-up confessionals.

But these archetypes were limiting, and though I believed that I could be some combination of Kristy, Mary Anne, Claudia, and Stacey, I didn't see anything remotely relatable in Dion and Twain. It was deeply important for me to establish a divide between Morissette and McLachlan versus Dion and Twain, to literally set my heroes apart from my enemies. I could only see the differences, stark and absolute, between the two pairs: great versus terrible, original versus derivative, important versus boring. I congratulated myself on having good taste, for being smarter than the masses who had yet to discover the intellectual and creative rewards of "alternative" culture. Of course, unbeknownst to me at the time, plenty of people, like Courtney Love, were condemning Morissette for being a sellout, mainstreaming alternative right out of existence. Sigh.

From where I stood, wearing the long-coveted Doc high-top boots that had given me blisters but were so worth it, Morissette and McLachlan were real artists and my feminist heroes, while Dion was a saccharine bloodsucker of vapid wonder and Twain was a tits-and-ass country crossover who personified the Madonna/whore complex. Those old, ugly thoughts were as much about policing my own body and shielding myself from vulnerability as they were about trying to contextualize my own surroundings and make space for myself in a fucked-up world that, through confoundingly contradictory media messaging and systemic aggressions, actively tried to break me down while simultaneously insisting I was more empowered than ever before.

***

Most youth and media share a certain similarity: an obsession with classification and articulating what should be obvious differences or similarities. John Hughes's classic high school film *The Breakfast Club* gave culture the quote that should have put an end to such impulses: "You see us as you want to see us: in the simplest terms, in the most convenient definitions. But what we found out is that each one of us is a brain, and an athlete, and a basket case, a princess, and a criminal." But it didn't.

Music genres do this, too. Even as artists try to resist categorization, the media and marketing teams are invested in simple terms with no room for deviation — all the easier to explain the music without using too many words. Rap, pop, rock, folk, punk, blues, country. Genre is a quick and dirty way to establish parameters and make things easily identifiable, but it doesn't allow for nuance or anomalies. There's a rigidity to partitioning what's cool and what's not, to insisting there is a shorthand to determine who ascribes to your taste and who doesn't. Parsing characteristics feels critical to your identity when you're fourteen or fifteen, and even if you're not always conscious of it, there's some intense truth-sorting that happens in those high school years as you begin to reject the inherited beliefs that have shaped you thus far and create your own philosophy. The hope, of course, is that we all learn more as we grow up and our worlds get a little (or a lot) bigger.

In 1993, I was fourteen years old and in the eighth grade. I lived with my family in an apartment above a drugstore in a building we called the Yellow Submarine. It was cramped quarters for four people. My thirteen-year-old sister and I shared one bedroom, which my father had to walk through to get to his, and my paternal grandmother slept in the living room. Our kitchen had black-and-white checkerboard linoleum. We had lived there since my parents split up a little more than two years earlier. Every night I opened the heavy curtain that covered my bedroom window and wrote novels (soapy, racy teen stories) by hand under the light from the streetlamp.

I knew I was a writer. Poetry came easily to me. My first poem was an ode to the electric keyboard I got as a Christmas present after my parents' split even though I'd never taken a single piano lesson. In school, English was my preferred subject thanks in part to our eighth-grade textbook. It contained short stories, grammar lessons, poetry, essays, and song lyrics from musicians. Before I'd ever heard Leonard Cohen's music, I fell in love with his poetry and the wild comparisons of "Bird on the Wire." Before I had a real sense of Joni Mitchell the singer, I cherished the unusual cadence of her words in my head and marvelled at the intoxicating beauty of "A Case of You." I didn't know that Janis Ian's "At Seventeen" was a song, not a poem. It was a revelation.

Though most of my friends at the time were losing their minds over New Kids on the Block, I had been devoted to the sweet pop sounds of Swedish duo Roxette since the age of eleven. But as most teenagers can attest, loving one thing often means hating another — enter Céline Dion. She was the first female musician I found myself vehemently rejecting. In retrospect, there's not a huge gulf between the two acts, but I was embracing my first feminist inclinations and rebelling against the notion that a woman needs a man and that love is the be all and end all that makes a woman's life worth living. Romance was dead. Matters of the heart were meant to be existential, devastating, and full of fire.

Dion's very existence as an artist was everything that was wrong with the world. I considered her weak and ridiculous. I didn't know the word "agency" at the time, but I knew she lacked something significant. Through Cohen and Mitchell and all the artists in my textbook, I had figured out what "real" music was, and Dion's vapid musings didn't compare.

Dion had no place in my heart or my mind, particularly in contrast to Sarah McLachlan, who came into my life around the same time. I was introduced to McLachlan when my friend Katrin made an appearance in one of her music videos, gallivanting in a field. Soon I was playing McLachlan's music on repeat. There was a sense of urgency in her words and a tension in her vocal range. She conveyed a desperate honesty, a darkness, and a sensuality that connected with every fibre of my fourteen-year-old self. McLachlan's music video for "Possession" was a softly lit feast of artfully naked flesh, Martha Stewart–esque white cotton sheet bondage, and Adam and Eve imagery, and her video for "Hold On" continued the moody lighting and light bondage, but this time with a circus contortionist twist. It was risqué, and at fourteen, I was definitely into sexy feelings even as I claimed to loathe romance.

When Shania Twain broke out in 1995 and her songs became inescapable, I found myself rolling my eyes and wanting to rip my ears off. She *needed* a man, and to my teenaged eyes, she was so obviously and overtly sexual: even in the music video for "(If You're Not in It for Love) I'm Outta Here!" Twain wears a red turtleneck but it's CROPPED to show her long expanse of impossibly toned abs. Every video seemed like it was all about Twain's perfect body and her teasing, coy flirtation with men. Even as she sang about putting men on notice, like "Any Man of Mine" or "Whose Bed Have Your Boots Been Under?," it felt like Twain was undermining her own lyrics and calling out mediocre dudes with music videos that seemed in service of the male gaze. She was Dion with a twang and fewer dramatics, but no less inauthentic in my eyes. Most offensive to me were her songs like "The Woman in Me (Needs the Man in You)" and "You Win My Love." They were empty and fluffy and encouraged girls to think only in terms of fairy tales and fantasies. They had nothing to do with real life. They felt like a "fuck you" to the burgeoning feminist in me. They were the sound of going backwards.

Alanis Morissette burst into my consciousness shortly after Shania. A cyclone of long dark hair, Alanis was fierce, vulnerable, and empowered. For the lost Canadian girls of the '90s who demanded more progressive role models, she was the alt-rock queen we'd been waiting for. Morissette was the one who would lead the revolution. She sang about men and love, too, but not in the same wimpy, cloying way of Dion and Twain. She was frank, direct, and more explicit in her sexuality, and I admired her candour. She spat out the twisted truth, hiding nothing, leaving nothing out, holding nothing back. I wanted somebody who would acknowledge how fucked up everything was, and that's what Morissette gave me.

Even within their archetypes, which were reiterated over and over in every Baby-Sitters Club book, the traits that distinguished Kristy, Mary Anne, Claudia, and Stacey blended and overlapped, criss-crossing into each other the way influences bleed between real people. From the beginning, I instinctively understood these characters represented familiar aspects of humanity. When I was older and women would debate their *Sex and the City* alter egos — "She's totally a Carrie. She's definitely a Charlotte. Slut, you're totally a Samantha! You? You wish you were Miranda." — I knew that they were all of us and we were all of them. *The Breakfast Club* already taught us that; wasn't anybody paying attention?

Yet I didn't afford that level of generous nuance to these four artists. In fact, all musicians were divided into those I liked, those I hated, and those I didn't think about at all. Perhaps it was because music felt so personal to me, while their personas were outsized, magnified, and extreme. I could see the common ground that McLachlan and Morissette occupied, as well as that shared by Dion and Twain, but in no way did I see any overlap across the enemy lines I'd established so definitively. Most emotionally intelligent people grow up to appreciate and recognize the ways in which rigid classification fails us with regard to the human condition, but my younger brain, which was still hungry for information and developing its own code of meaning, needed to first divide people into a binary of good and bad. I didn't yet understand how binary thinking can be a way of harming one's self by excluding what's "other."

Similarly, a substantial amount of pop culture media does its best to reduce every celebrity to their lowest common denominators. Great writers colour in the space between the labels, but all too often it comes down to the most simplistic terms with which to describe (and judge) people: gay or straight, fat or thin, crazy or sane, and so on. Consider this 1995 review of *Jagged Little Pill* by David Browne for *Entertainment Weekly*:

> Spiteful and seething, Alanis Morissette's "You Oughta Know" turns jealous bile into something worth hearing. Over a throbbing-gristle beat that grabs your collar and rips it off, the Canadian newcomer unleashes her rage at a lover who dumped her for another, threatening to disrupt dinner. . . .
>
> The rest of Morissette's touted U.S. debut album, *Jagged Little Pill*, is much harder to swallow. What sounds arresting on a single grows wearing over a full album. Producer-co-songwriter Glen Ballard's arrangements are clunky mixtures of alternative mood music and hammy arena rock, and the 21-year-old Morissette tends to wildly oversing every other line. And what lines: In her songs, men take her for granted and mentally abuse her, and she retaliates by threatening to leave one of her exes' names off her album credits (talk about a career-minded individual). Morissette needs to make new friends. C+[1]

Here Browne only lightly invokes the Madonna and Mary Magdalene tropes that are still universally weaponized against

1 David Browne, "Jagged Little Pill," *Entertainment Weekly*, August 4, 1995, https://ew.com/article/1995/08/04/jagged-little-pill/.

women, but they're still evident. Morissette is, of course, no virtuous mother but is instead "spiteful and seething." And apparently all of her songs are about men taking her for granted or abusing her mentally? Is this yet another instance of a reviewer telling on himself, yelping when a song pokes at his own misogyny or the way he has treated women in his relationships? Hard to say. But good girl or bad girl; virgin or whore; nice and polite or raging bitch — in patriarchal math, these are two sides of the same lady coins. Most women even buy into it themselves. I certainly have. And though intellectually most of us realize it's crap, the duality has seeped so far into many women's identities that we can't divorce ourselves from it without concentrated effort.

Everybody knew that McLachlan and Dion were the "good girls" and Twain and Morissette were the "bad girls." But what I couldn't see was that the enemy lines were constantly being breached and nothing stayed in the rigid balance I had grown so attached to. Morissette singing about blow jobs didn't faze me. I was excited about the reality of it all, even if I had zero sexual experience beyond figuring out masturbation and managing my own pleasure. To my mascaraed eyes, Twain's bare midriffs, on the other hand, struck me as cheap and unfeminist. I saw nothing hypocritical in my assessment. I called it as I saw it. Twain had to take her clothes off to make a point. Her looks and her sexuality were as integral to her success as any actual talent. Morissette was the real deal, the antithesis to Twain in every way — except she wasn't, with an image that was just as carefully curated by her record label, her management, even the VJs who announced her videos on TV. The categories and divisions I (and many others) had imposed on them lulled us into accepting a limited and limiting world view as truth. I didn't know then that we were witnessing a seismic shift and these four women were going to change Canadian music forever. I didn't know that all four of these artists would ultimately come to occupy the same space in Canada's pop culture: icons, best-selling artists, punchlines. I didn't believe that I was part of the problem, but I absolutely was.

Confronting my own complicity has been a rigorous exercise. It has forced me to wrestle with who I was, who I had always hoped to be, and who I'm actively trying to become. I'm gentle with my foolishness, the all-in, righteous certainty that I once held fast and dear. But I'm not protective or defensive of it any longer. As I write these words and more deeply consider my accountability, I know there's so much more to say. The last decade has seen a larger cultural reckoning about the sexist, misogynist, racist, ableist, and toxic treatment of many high-profile women by the media, fans, and general public. The result has been features, interviews, essays, and documentaries asking variations on the question "Do we owe *x* an apology?"

X has been Britney Spears, Pamela Anderson, TLC, Janet Jackson, Monica Lewinsky, and countless other '90s-era stars whose reputations, mental and physical wellness, and livelihoods seemed to melt in that relentless onslaught of paparazzi flashes, clickbait harassment, rampant racism, cruel speculation, assumptions, and accusations. What feels different now than in 2015, when the first edition of this book was published, is that there's more cultural interest in accountability and how these women were treated, and many women themselves are reclaiming their agency. We're hearing from them directly, often for the first time, and the indictments are clear. Exploitation, extraction, and erasure were factors and will continue to be until we address that it's all fruit of the original poisoned tree: powerful and wealthy men like Clive Davis, Jeff Bezos, and Rupert Murdoch who control the record labels, the streaming services, the tabloid magazines, even the photo agencies, and who have built barrier after barrier designed to prevent these women from using their undiluted voices.

My fat body is not normative; it's rebellious in its lush rolls and unapologetically pleasurable fullness. I also grew up in a poor/lower-working-class home and have never quite outgrown the class panic and precarity that ruled my youth and young adult years. But my privileges are robust and clear. Straight, white, cis women like me benefit from white supremacy, homophobia, and transphobia. And if my feminism isn't intersectional, anti-racist, trans-inclusive, class-inclusive, and actively participating in decolonization, and disability justice, I'm just upholding the dusty, decaying bones of the patriarchy. I've been complicit in my own ruin and oppression, but I'm working hard to unlearn everything I've internalized. I'm so grateful to be part of this era of cultural reassessment, to identify and acknowledge all of the shitty ways that misogyny, sexism, and gendered stereotypes — externalized and internalized — have caused so much harm and done so much damage.

In retrospect, coming of age in the era of Dion, Twain, Morissette, and McLachlan meant a wild array of influences and images. But their archetypes loomed over every aspect of my youth, representing four different genres of music, four different faces of Canada, and four different corners of my burgeoning feminism and my internalized sexism. It's just a coincidence that their five-year ascent overlapped with my formative high school years, and it's taken me a long time — arguably too long — to realize I was watching history being made and witnessing the greatest moment of womens empowerment the Canadian music industry has ever seen. Do we owe Dion, Twain, Morissette, and McLachlan apologies? I know I owe a few and that the culture does, too. Based on the research I conducted to update this book, I know there have been many reappraisals of their music, work, and public personae in the last decade. All four have also experienced significant comebacks, setbacks, and reinventions. Yet these wildly successful artists are often still punchlines. There are still debates about the quality of their songs, challenges to their musicianship, all barbs that have their roots in sexism and misogyny. Their successes, though real, valid, and record-breaking, continue to be minimized and/or erased in favour of "better" artists, which is far too often code for male artists.

Actually, fuck it. We're beyond apologies. It's time to atone.

MAKING PEACE WITH CÉLINE DION

Mockery, Manipulation, and Matters of the Heart

When you come of age in the time of Céline Dion, growing up takes on a certain sateen sheen.

Falling in love, first kisses, subsequent breakups, and inevitable pregnancy scares: every moment has a song, if not an entire soundtrack. And if these milestones happened between 1991 and 1999, Dion and her emotionally wrought, soaring soprano melodramas likely played in the background. (Anyone born between 1993 and 1995, if you're reading this right now, go ahead and do the math: yes, you were probably conceived thanks to Dion and "The Power of Love." On behalf of Canada, you're welcome.)

Shortly after making her English-language debut, Dion claimed a place amongst the reigning pop divas of her time. She stood shoulder to shoulder with Whitney Houston and Mariah Carey in terms of vocal range and power. Her goal was stardom, and you could both hear and feel that ambition in every note; she wrung all the feelings from your senses, leaving you a dry, dirty mop of human emotion. It's appropriate that Dion is simultaneously one of the most mocked and most beloved singers in the world. Her voice packs an ocean's worth of feeling and sentiment into every word, and she has made a career out of using her elemental pipes to sell the most treacly, generic adult contemporary pop.

The shrewdness of her business skills are balanced with genuine talent and Dion's instincts are flawless. The sales numbers for every record since 1993's *The Colour of My Love* (twenty to thirty million worldwide) have reaffirmed Dion as master of the heart.[1] She places herself firmly in the middle of our biggest romantic thrills and our most heartbroken moments, singing about our deepest fears and wildest hopes. Love is her business, but because love is such a human construct, we are both her commodities and her consumers.

I think this is where my initial resentment started to build: I didn't begrudge her ascent to pop stardom, but I did resent what felt like relentless emotional manipulation song after song, sameness after sameness, calculating David Foster ballad after calculating Diane Warren ballad. The earnestness in her artifice was hard for me to reconcile when I was fourteen. Now, having seen the graceless rise of "music" that demands quotation marks around it because it's so fake, unoriginal, and overproduced (sorry, Black Eyed Peas, Ashlee Simpson, Kevin Federline, and Maroon 5), I've come to appreciate Dion in a new way.

Early on, I couldn't turn a blind eye to what I perceived as Dion's crass commercialism and the non-stop marketing machine that twisted her into a larger-than-life diva. Magazines like *Maclean's* and *People* splashed her face on their covers. Hit

1 David Ball, "This Week in History, December 12 to 18," Canadian Music Hall of Fame, https://web.archive.org/web/20140929172529/http://canadianmusichalloffame.ca/this-week-in-history-december-12-to-18/.

songs featured in blockbuster films like *Beauty and the Beast* and *You've Got Mail* kickstarted her ubiquity on radio, MuchMusic, and MTV. Soon enough, she was being compared to icons Barbra Streisand and Whitney Houston. I couldn't comprehend the fevered, frantic love of Dion's dedicated fandom, from the reports of millions screaming and sobbing at her sold-out world tours to the hardcore obsessives who flocked in the hundreds to stand outside her wedding venue to witness, even in passing, the spectacle of all that white lace up close. Their thirst matched her thirst, and all I could do was wince and cringe. It was certainly never cool in the contemporary sense of the word to like Céline Dion, but that's likely why so many people are compelled to such devotional heights: her unapologetic, guileless earnestness.

It is precisely because of this earnestness that her music makes me feel things it doesn't necessarily earn. There's no real reason I should get teary listening to "My Heart Will Go On." I don't like *Titanic*. I thought the ending was stupid, and that piece of wood was easily big enough for them both. The tin whistle at the beginning of the song is cloying, as is the whispery little girl voice Dion uses to softly pull us in. And yet she slips inside her character so completely, damned if I don't believe that her heart really will go on and yours will, too. When the final verse crescendoes and she asserts that there's nothing to be afraid of because her love is beside her, well, it's shattering. And it's supposed to be. So well played, Ms. Dion, consider me willingly gamed.

There's passion in Dion's songs, but it's a sexless passion, like a Ken doll's beige genital wasteland. It may be considered pretentious, but it's actually wholly accessible. There's no sly, arch abstraction to a Dion ballad. It's perfectly devoid of subtext. It's entertaining and emotional, it goes down easy, and its sole purpose can be the amplification of the listener's own feelings, whatever those are. It doesn't bring any agenda other than "FEEL THIS. FEEL IT NOW."

Despite her lyrical interpretations of love devolving into meaningless platitudes, it's impossible to deny how much Dion means to her fans, even now, decades into her career. She affords the listener permission to pull down the walls and let something enter in a safe, risk-free way. That's huge. So many of us are taught to deny, suppress, and suffocate the most basic emotional reactions every day. We live guided by arbitrary and not-so-arbitrary rules: codes of conduct at work, societal constructions, neighbourhoods, elevators. Never mind the more oppressive conditions of socio-economics, gender, race, and sexuality.

But it's not the songs themselves or the production that earn these feelings: it's Dion. Dion the vocalist, performer, and pop diva construct wants to touch people, build safe spaces for them to emote alongside her. It's not selfless, but it's not predatory, either; she wants their adulation and adoration, but she also wants them to feel as moved by music and love as she is. She's spreading the gospel of Big, Epic Feelings that can change people with the power of her voice. She's a skilled woman who has perfected her instrument, carved a precise path for her career, and never wavered. She basks in the worship and adulation of generations of people who are grateful for the singularity of her vision, her commitment to being a conduit for life's biggest moments. The secret to her soft manipulation is her sincerity, and it's in this way that her songs own some of the biggest moments in our lives. This is Dion's superpower, and it's why her music endures; as principal shareholder of our nostalgia, she lays claim to our pasts and to pieces of our hearts, even if we sometimes resent the fuck out of her for it, as I do, in my darker moments.

As a teen who was cultivating a more indie-focused (and less "mainstream" or basic) personality, I objected strenuously and righteously to everything I felt Dion represented: banal melodrama, terrible clichés about women, songs that were essentially gold-plated crap. I saw her peddling and hustling to reinforce gender stereotypes, a woman with obvious daddy issues who served to please her decades-older husband, a woman so invested in a *Pygmalion* transformation she found her own Professor Higgins, but even worse. I didn't deny her talent, but I devalued it. I judged, harshly, the friends who worshipped her rather than someone like Courtney Love or Jann Arden. There were women who wrote their own music and had something to say, who weren't content to simply sing somebody else's words. Or so I thought.

I wonder now why I've always placed such value on singers writing their own songs; I don't require actors to write their own material or any other artist to be entirely DIY, and yet there's something about songwriting, the craftsmanship and the creation process, that is tied so intimately to the actual singing. I value those words and the arrangements almost more than I value the vocals.

But, like everyone, I just couldn't escape Dion's soaring voice.

Like Twain, for almost a decade, she was everywhere and in everything, and it was just too much. The cross-border success in America amplified Dion's cross-media reach, too, from radio to film and television. In 1993, Dion scored her first #1 hit in America with "The Power of Love." (It was also #1 in Canada.) In 1996, she did it again with "Because You Loved Me," which was also the theme song for the Michelle Pfeiffer and Robert Redford hit romantic film *Up Close & Personal*. She won Grammy Awards and Juno Awards and performed live on television at the opening ceremony of the 1996 summer Olympics in Atlanta. She was in my friends' CD players and in our school choir repertoire; her voice rang out in every shopping mall, grocery store, and high school dance. And then came *Titanic*. Dion was inescapable. In a 1996 *Billboard* interview, John Doelp, executive VP of 550/Sony, Dion's label, put it this way: "Her typical consumer? Life to death. She has transcended any kind of demographic study. At her shows, you see the family, the date, the parents, the kids and the teenagers."[2] From cradle to coffin, Dion has you covered.

Ubiquity can sometimes feel akin to bullying. The relentless repetition starts to feel like oppression or harassment, which then triggers resentment, irritation, and rage. This may be why people reacted so viscerally and with so much contempt to something as relatively innocuous as someone singing with gusto. Of course, there were those who hated Dion because she was a woman singing with so much command and presence; sexism and misogyny plagued her, as well as some anti-Québécois and anti-French sentiment. Millions of people found ways to justify making Dion the object of their collective displeasure, but the honest truth was Dion could fucking sing. And that's what matters.

---

2 Chuck Taylor, "550's Celine Dion Takes Stardom to Next Level," *Billboard*, November 9, 1996.

Dion's raw vocal talent was, and is, impossible to deny, but I was willfully oblivious to it as a teen. I couldn't see the commitment or drive, the singularity of her vision. The overarching truth, the one that takes precedence over every other narrative, is that Dion worked her ass off. By 1993, when she became an inescapable part of my youth, she'd already released eleven albums, nine in French and two in English. At the age of twenty-five, Dion was a veteran of the music industry with more albums under her belt than most artists release in an entire career. This is Dion's other greatest asset: an incredible work ethic. She wanted it. Badly. Always.

The youngest of fourteen children, Dion was born and raised in Charlemagne, Québec, poor but happily singing with her family and performing alongside her siblings in her parents' bar. At twelve, Dion's brother Jacques recorded her and dropped off a tape for René Angélil, a music manager, who invited her to audition for him in person. After their roughly thirty-five years in the business together, the story is pretty much legend, but she sang and he cried, and he subsequently mortgaged his home to finance her first record, taking Dion and her mother on the road throughout Canada, Europe, and Japan.

Her debut album, *La voix du bon Dieu* (*The Good Lord's Voice*), came out in 1981 and features a few co-writing credits for Dion and various family members. The following year, she released *Tellement j'ai d'amour . . .* (*I Have So Much Love . . .*) and dropped out of school at age fourteen to pursue music full-time. The timeline of Dion's triumphs, milestones, and eyebrow-raising moments came fast and furious between 1983 and 1993. Already a star in Québec, Dion became the first Canadian to score a gold record in France. In 1984, she performed for Pope John Paul II during his visit to Canada, and by 1985, Dion had released her seventh French-language record. Meanwhile, Angélil divorced his second wife.

Dion competed in international singing competitions, and at eighteen, she saw Michael Jackson in concert and told Angélil she wanted to be a star like Jackson. She was still a teenager while Angélil, who was twenty-six years her senior, was already her secret boyfriend (they had started dating in 1987), as well as her manager. Angélil, whom she described as being "like a second father" on *Regis and Kathie Lee* in 1990, determined that if she wanted to be a superstar, the answer was fixing her physical appearance so Dion retreated from the public for several months for dental surgery (the only confirmed of her many rumoured surgeries). Dion's eventual career was her dream come true, so the transformation worked, or at least didn't hurt. However, I will always bristle at the pervasive notion that women need to look a certain way and conform to certain Western, white beauty standards, even if they're as naturally gifted and tenacious as Dion.

In addition to having the rumoured cosmetic procedures, Dion also spent time improving her language skills in anticipation of her English-language debut, 1990's *Unison*. The album's biggest single "Where Does My Heart Beat Now" began to soar up the charts. The following year, she and Peabo Bryson performed the theme song for Disney's *Beauty and the Beast*; after their performance and win at the sixty-fourth Academy Awards, intergenerational Dion fandom was officially underway. They won both an Oscar and a Grammy, and Dion credited the film with putting her on the "map" and giving her a "name": "I will always be thankful to that song for giving me a career."[3] The song was featured on Dion's self-titled 1992 album, which also spawned a few hit singles and prompted the *Chicago Tribune* to declare that Dion had "clearly joined Mariah Carey and Whitney Houston as one of the premier voices on the pop scene."[4]

But she was also battling detractors who claimed that her voice was technically proficient but lacked heart, and that her English concerts were awkward affairs, markedly different experiences than those offered in French by "la p'tite Québécoise." A 1992 *Maclean's* article offered insight into how those language difficulties had perhaps distorted the English-speaking world's understanding of Dion as an artist. In French, Dion was known for her passion, wit, and a "rollicking" sense of humour, and it was acknowledged that her French material was more substantial and less about love and loss. The English concerts were a less fluid, more rehearsed experience, attributable, perhaps, to her linguistic discomfort and self-admitted perfectionism. Said Dion: "I have to pretend I am a strong person. But really I am so afraid of making a mistake."[5]

3 Isabelle Khoo, "Celine Dion Says 'Beauty and the Beast' Put Her on the Map," *Huffington Post*, January 20, 2017, https://www.huffpost.com/archive/ca/entry/celine-dion-says-beauty-and-the-beast-put-her-on-the-map_n_14284210.

4 "Memos - n Home Entertainment . . . Rave Recordings. Jan DeKnock: [NORTH SPORTS FINAL Edition]," *Chicago Tribune*, May 21, 1992.

5 E.K. Fulton, "Queen Celine," *Maclean's*, June 1, 1992.

A fair number of critics loved Dion's music, but a substantial portion toed a very weird line of praising her skill while simultaneously putting her down. *People*'s Jeremy Helligar opened his review of *The Colour of My Love* by lamenting how tough it was becoming "to tell today's pop ingenues apart." He continued, "The third U.S. release from French-Canadian songbird Dion could be the latest from Mariah Carey. Same power pipes. Same department-store song selection: spotless ballads on the ground floor, a few dance tunes upstairs, and a mid-tempo toe-tapper or two riding the escalator." But then he flipped a switch, criticizing the "vocal somersaults" of Carey's songs while saying that Dion "quietly makes mushy blather sound like gospel."[6] It's very backhanded praise, but praise nonetheless; in the '90s, it almost always came at the expense of pitting two women against each other.

The Colour of My Love was also a coming out of sorts. Dion dedicated the album to Angélil and admitted that they'd been in a romantic relationship since 1987 and engaged since 1991. Heavy hints had been revealed in numerous interviews, including the 1992 *Maclean's* cover story, "Queen Celine," in which Dion acknowledged that she had a "significant" man in her life. The article also included this telling paragraph:

> The degree of Dion's dependence on her manager was evident in New York. Discovering in the hotel lobby that she had neither the number nor the key to her suite, she lamented: "I have never checked into a room myself. I don't know how

6 Jeremy Helligar, "Picks & Pans: Song," *People*, February 28, 1994.

> to even order room service." Still, the resilience of their partnership surfaced on May 7 in Los Angeles when the workaholic Angélil suffered a heart attack. It was Dion who took control. She put him into a taxi and they went to a hospital. That evening, she flew alone and in tears to New York and then to Europe to continue the promotional tour (Angélil is currently recuperating at home in Montreal). Interviewed in Paris by the Quebec weekly *7 Jours*, Dion said: "I feel like a car without an engine. Rene is the engine of my life and, without him, there are things I simply can't figure out."

The age difference got attention, but it didn't affect record sales. The album became her best-selling record to date. It also firmly established Dion's enduring relationships with songwriters and producers David Foster and Diane Warren while proving that producer Ric Wake would always steer her wrong and, above all, that love was the servant and Dion its master.

The Colour of My Love opens with Dion's cover of "The Power of Love," easily the strongest song on the record, and she absolutely makes it her own (sorry to the original singer, Jennifer Rush). Dion uses every vocal trick in her arsenal: the lift of her soprano; the curious, quiet tentativeness to her delivery as the song opens; the lilt of her French accent; the slight nasal curl to some of the soft ways she hugs her longer vowels. Her voice takes on a bit of scratch and an almost lusty urgency. The vocal acrobatics smash everything around them, like Miss Piggy in full meltdown on any given episode of *The Muppet Show*.

But the interesting thing about Dion is that she resisted sonic consistency across the album. There's no major through line here; rather, there are sidesteps into R&B-lite, like "Misled." Dion never quite finds her footing on the track, and words like "dissed" are almost comical coming out of her French Canadian mouth. Dion always seemed much older when she was in her mid-twenties, so the youthful vernacular sounds and feels awkward.

"Think Twice" revisits "Power of Love" territory, and Dion shows that she is born for the theatrical — that deliberate and delicate push-pull between her tender whisper and her full thrust diva vocal flair. But just as quickly, there's another sidestep, this time into the '80s-esque "Only One Road," which sounds like something Barbra Streisand might have pounced on given the chance. The song serves a dual audience with lyrics that lend themselves to the style of a Christian anthem that celebrates the "one road" she must walk and a faithful devotion to an unnamed figure to whom she must return. As the super successful child of Roman Catholic parents with a huge family, it's easy to see how Dion would have been embraced by people of faith and why she and her team wouldn't think twice about exploiting that. She rarely talks about sex directly in her songs, preferring euphemisms and matters of the heart as opposed to sins of the flesh (as it were).

"Love Doesn't Ask Why" reveals Dion's future musical tells: whispery, shimmery moments brushing up against huge, bombastic choruses that surge out of nowhere and backup singers filling up the space around the star as she freestyles and emotes up and down the melodic scale. Oddly it wasn't a single, and it's certainly more of a deep cut, but it's so indicative of the formula she was beginning to map out for herself that I'm surprised this song wasn't a bigger deal in 1993.

The record ends not with a bang but with a puddle of sentiment. "No Living without Loving You" is a deceptively upbeat song about how she'd die without her man. But musically it's quite dated for 1993, like a woman's powersuit from *Dynasty*, all shoulder pads and primary color, standing out in stark contrast against a sea of short flowered dresses. The production relies heavily on '80s-style cheery synths and shimmery percussion, while the lyrics never go any deeper than the title, with its heteronormative devotion, indicates. The final two songs, plus "Lovin' Proof" and the title track, further support the notion that single-girl status is a fate worse than death in Dion's world. If this record came out today, three tracks would still be huge and everything else would tank. It's simply not a cohesive album or listening experience, and there are precious few moments of exaltation and significance.

In 1994, Dion and Angélil married in Quebec in a lavish ceremony — seriously, it was like Quebec's version of a royal wedding. They hosted five hundred guests, and the bride was adorned in an ostentatious headdress made with two thousand Swarovski crystals that stood almost a foot off her scalp and weighed more than six pounds.[7] Two years later, Dion released *Falling into You*, another blockbuster. It was also another overstuffed album, but it was bolstered by enough hit-song highs that

7 Marie Périer, "Flashback: Céline Dion's 1994 Wedding in Vintage Photos," *Vogue France*, April 9, 2020, https://www.vogue.fr/wedding/article/thowback-celine-dion-rene-angelil-1994-wedding-in-vintage-images.

the head-scratching lows failed to impact Dion's album sales. She was talented, yes, but she was also at least five percent lucky to come to prominence during the height of the CD boom rather than a decade later when streaming, and the ease with which we can now listen to single tracks instead of whole albums, would obliterate record sales.

And while she was at the top of the sales charts, there were also plenty of detractors who continued to contrast Dion with other multi-octave "divas" of the era, insisting Dion's voice was proficient but cold, and that she was just a robot rushing out the hit singles without any heart or soul as compared to the likes of Mariah Carey, Whitney Houston, or Barbra Streisand. Dion was always affronted by this assessment, and in various interviews she has reaffirmed that her tenacity is about her own expectations of perfection, not some kind of imagined competition with other top-notch pop stars. "I don't work hard to sell; I work hard because I have to work hard," she told *Entertainment Weekly* in 1996. "I want to be the best of me."[8]

"Falling into You," the album's title track, is utterly forgettable, which makes it two records in a row where the titular song has been among the album's weakest. Dion disagreed, talking at length in her biography, *Céline Dion: For Keeps*, about her pride in that song. Dissatisfied with the original arrangements, Dion fought to re-record it to be more in keeping with her vision, stating, "This song marked a step of my emancipation as an artist . . . I was becoming a mature, grown-up, autonomous artist."[9] It's clear

8 Jeff Gordinier, "Celine Dion Takes on America," *Entertainment Weekly*, March 29, 1996, https://ew.com/article/1996/03/29/celine-dion-takes-america/.

9 Jenna Glatzer, *Céline Dion: For Keeps* (Kansas City: Andrews McMeel Pub, 2005).

that she felt a sense of achievement, a sense of authority in her voice. But it's also frustrating that this is the sound for which she was fighting. Dion's instincts tend towards schmaltz rather than sophistication, which is both a gift and a burden. Unfortunately, it also has one of the grossest sax solos in the history of sax solos, low and aiming for sultry but landing at a sleazy kind of stank. It doesn't help that the accompanying music video features numerous clowns and old-timey circus acts. At one point, Dion stares into the camera unblinking as a clown affixes a wig to her head. The aforementioned sax solo scores a scene of Dion standing in the foreground, sidestage in a long wig and purple cape as circus clowns flip acrobatically in the background.

"It's All Coming Back to Me Now" is one of her best songs, and a personal favorite, even if it's for all the wrong reasons. I love that it sounds like a rejected Meat Loaf ballad (and, guess what: Meat Loaf was the one rejected when his frequent collaborator gave it to Dion to release first). I adore mini-operas and story songs, particularly ones that are drenched in gothic-light bombast; I'm a sucker for huge, over-the-top crescendos that suddenly drop into quiet depths. It's like a rainy night that turns into a howling, growling storm: thunder and lightning everywhere, trees felled, power grids snapping the sky with bright white flashes. And then suddenly it's all gone. Nature stretches, flexes, lashes out, and is calm again. That's this song.

It's the unfolding of a love story that's theatrical, epic, and all-consuming — the kind of love story that feels much more believable with this song than any of the others on this album. Maybe it's the sadness and the innate grief entrenched in every word that makes "It's All Coming Back to Me Now" more palatable than the next track, itself another huge blockbuster.

"Because You Loved Me" is a gentler, sweeter, simpler love song that lets the listener breathe a bit after the marathon of the album opener. But I detested its sentiment and lyrics as a teenager. Frankly, I still do, though I understand it and interpret it far less literally now. But as Dion sings about how she's nothing without "him" — maybe another worship song doubling as a love song? — I always feel exhausted. *Goddamn, girl, get a sense of self,* I used to think.

"Make You Happy" is a Ric Wake–produced track, and fittingly, this is the first terrible song on the record. Dion is devoid of funk, but every time she works with Wake, he attempts to shoehorn her into the same mould that worked for his other artists like Whitney Houston, Mariah Carey, and Taylor Dayne. I don't know whether Dion desperately wanted to be cooler than she was, or if Wake had no other style he could work in, but it's emblematic of the problem with divas and albums. Divas demand tent pole songs, singles, and huge standout numbers, not necessarily cohesive, consistent, quality albums that build thematically and sonically over a tracklist. A variety of producers and multiple songwriters aren't always capable of crafting a package that both coalesces and showcases a diva in multiple ways. Instead the listener gets shot around like a pinball, bouncing off bumpers and flippers, careening up and down (emotional) ramps to nowhere, and trying to make sense of the frenzy.

"Seduces Me" is an interesting torch song, but it's the antithesis of the Dion construct we're most often presented with: emotional, voluminous, in love and loving, but never sexual. Her persona could approach sexy but only in a sterile, performative, overly mannered way. This is her first English-language song in which Dion manages to convey desire and convincingly communicate her very human longing. The Spanish guitar helps, as does her full-throated attack on the crescendo. Plus there's a certain charm in the way her Québécoise accent slips through in her over-enunciation of the word "seduce." For all the soap-opera-esque elements at work, this feels like Dion at her most vulnerable and fallible rather than perfect and poised.

"All by Myself" packs a lifetime of blue moons into its slight structure. The song itself has all the finesse of a child's popsicle-stick birdhouse, but Dion treats it like a monument of great import, transcending the material even if she doesn't quite transform it. Her voice is robust and strong, even in her solitude, and she never caves to the anguish of her loneliness. She is defiantly rejecting it and asking for what she needs. This is how she makes bad songs good — it's not karaoke but ownership. There's a visceral experience, which permits Dion to be seen as a creator even when she's not. Her artistic impressions define her, for better or for worse.

It's impossible, though, to fathom how Dion and her people could listen to "All by Myself" and then sequence the next three songs without major pause for thought. The quality is simply not there on the vapid, Wake-produced (of course) "Declaration of Love," the equally schmaltzy "Dreamin' of You," and the icing on the treacle layer cake, "I Love You."

"If That's What It Takes" pivots and revisits the breathy Dion vocals that always make me want to smash my head against a wall. Everything about the song is the equivalent of a Lifetime movie, from the water-drop sound effects and synths layered atop percussive clicks to Dion's urgent, breathy delivery, an over-the-top performance in lieu of substance. It's pleasurable as a passing entertainment, and it sounds fine as long as you don't pay too much attention. It certainly doesn't require or reward analytical listening or critical thinking. In fact, it actively punishes those things. Just turn your brain off and enjoy it. That's the magic of Dion.

The final three tracks have so little in common, they could be found on three separate albums. But they're not, of course; they're all right here. "I Don't Know" is the English-language version of her song "Je sais pas," from the French-language album she released in 1995. It's better in French, though both feature a particularly dated '80s-style sax solo that pushes the song into joke territory rather than an effective, gritty, bluesy number.

Her cover of "River Deep, Mountain High" is a showstopper, but the arrangement and her performance feel like a lot of work. You can practically hear the sweat on her forehead as she attacks the chorus. It's huge, full of energy, and begging for a flood of spotlights, like an opening number to a Las Vegas revue show, perhaps, a hint at what was to come a decade or so later when Dion's residency sparked a spectacular revival of the city's concert scene.

The final track on the Canadian edition, "Your Light," is the least Dion-sounding track — in fact, with the "Yeah!" growl, kick-start drums, and Dion singing in her lower register, it sounds like a Shania Twain reject — an utterly bizarre way to close a record since it's simply confusing for the listener. But it's catchy. Her delivery snaps like the whip of a wet towel, and it feels like she's playing dress-up. This was the era of Garth Brooks and his nonsensical alter ego Chris Gaines (a persona that Brooks briefly adopted to sing emo-pop songs while wearing a shaggy black wig with bangs that hung into his eyes and sporting a soul patch), so it's possible that Dion had a plan to use this platform to launch a new identity. But whatever excitement or energy is generated is quickly subsumed by the unfortunate realization that "Your Light" is in keeping, lyrically, with most of the themes on the album: being everything for a man; a man being everything for her; and a substantial lack of independent identity, of knowing herself, of articulating who she is versus who she is in relation to a man.

Those things that I found so frustrating in high school persist and are why I still find it difficult to fully embrace the majority of her music, even if my opinions around Dion as an artist have changed. It's also the baggage that I bring to the table. I'm happily married and madly in love. It's the kind of love where literally every time we ride the elevator alone together, we kiss. Every single elevator ride essentially since we met in 2006. We live in an apartment building. It's a lot of kissing, though the pandemic and mask-wearing put a dent in the ongoing count. But even a person like me, who finally understands the extraordinary expansion of one's life when she falls in love, can't stomach Dion's penchant for songs that deprioritize her own identity so substantially.

Dion's music emphasizes society's lack of gender equality, but it's not her problem to fix. She can sing about love in whatever permutation she supports. If love to Dion is a tidal wave of personal sacrifices of her identity, well, that's her experience, possibly quite literally. After all, she was the youngest of fourteen children, growing up in abject poverty, but she had the undeniable gift of her voice coupled with a belief that she could be more. At twelve years old, she met a man twenty-six years her senior who believed in her so wholly that he mortgaged his home to help make her a star. Fourteen years later, she married this man who had given up everything to focus on her.

In most of her songs, at least throughout the '90s, Dion presents as this figure of arrested development: stalled forever emotionally as a young girl who's totally and entirely shaped by the older man who believed in her, took her out of a crowded house, and said, "Yes, you're special." Dion is a smart woman, operating with her own agency, but in 2015, at least to me, it seemed that she crafted her entire existence around this mountain of a man. She put somebody else at the center of her own universe, was orbiting around him, and sang about it. After all, as she told *7 Jours*, without Angélil, she was "a car without an engine."

Ignoring the optics of it all (and the potentially predatory nature of the entire relationship — we weren't there, we don't know, but yes, I'm still squicked out), Dion's earlier understanding of love was entirely wrapped up in sacrifice, sweeping romantic gestures, and defying the odds. It was escapist fantasy — romance novels disguised as three-minute songs and delivered with one of the most distinctive, compelling, and identifiable voices of the twentieth century.

My first real "situation" with a boy came about when I was fifteen. I loved him in an angsty, drama-ridden, self-loathing way. Our dynamic mirrored the fictional relationships I so admired, ones that were passionately cerebral. It was an entirely chaste situation (until years later when it wasn't), but it was combustible and affectionate. Always close friends, I pushed way harder for us to be something more than he ever did. I was a fat, artsy girl. He was a skinny, nerdy boy, and our relationship emulated all my go-tos: the flirty, prickly tension between Jo and George on *The Facts of Life*; the fiery, combative sparring of *Cheers'* Sam and Diane; the gentle toxicity between Miss Piggy and Kermit. I kept looking at couples whose shorthand was banter, sarcasm, fighting, arguing, and debating, and I convinced myself that those were the dynamics of a typical relationship. If you argue enough, you eventually fall in love, because love and hate, right? I wanted Alanis Morissette's version of love, or Sarah McLachlan's version of love, anything but the placid, weepy, ill-advised platitudes of a Céline Dion song.

The greatest sin of Dion's songbook is its tireless beating of the "love = forever" drum. It's, of course, fine to want to believe love is forever, but the language that we use to bind one to the other is intensely problematic. I know that forever is very real for some people. My father never stopped loving my mother. Ever. It was just who he was. In retrospect, I wish now he had fallen in love with someone else, but he never did. She left him for another man — he worked for my father — and it was complicated and messy. I have a clearer picture of my dad's resolute nature and silent, unobtrusive grief than I do of what their marriage was actually like. Of course it couldn't last. They were practically children when they got together, and my father had only ever craved stability while that's all my mother had ever known in her own family. Theirs was a relationship steeped in tiny class warfare — my mother was accustomed to certain middle-class comforts and was always in the shadow of her elders who possessed notions of family money, such as it was, whereas my father had been on his own since he was fourteen.

But he loved her. And he loved my sister and me. And they made co-parenting work in their own way. We lived with Dad and my grandma, but he continued to come with us to family dinners at my mom's and with my mom's family. We all celebrated Christmas, birthdays, and family holidays together, every year. My sister and I liked it better when he was there, and he never shied away from that, never let it be known that maybe he felt too humiliated or too judged or that he wanted to be anywhere else. They made our lives as normal as possible. Instead of Mom and Dad, it was Mom and her new partner, and Dad. So simple, right? But I knew it was hard for him. It was probably hard for my mom, too, but she had a partner there to help her.

I always wondered why Dad wasn't angrier. He never badmouthed her to us, not once. I didn't fully understand that he still loved her until a few years later. I remember us eating dinner at a Chinese restaurant one night in December when he said suddenly, almost out of the blue, "Happy anniversary to me." It was still their wedding anniversary, no matter what had happened. When love ends for one person, where does the other person put theirs? They either let it go, like a balloon chasing the sky, or suffocate under its weight, a landslide coming down a mountain.

When we operate under a belief in forever love, romantic or platonic, we fool ourselves into believing it isn't conditional. All love is conditional — love exists between two people as a condition of each person feeling that love separately. You can't love somebody enough to make them love you back, nor can you love somebody enough to make up for how little they love you.

We teach kids from a young age that forever is easy, a tangible result of good behaviour or DNA or just what comes at the end of the story, the happily ever after everybody fumbles towards. Intimate and platonic BFFs are what we're all searching for, and when you find them, it's amazing. This is no slight on any forever relationship that lasts, but it's the cult of forever that screws us all up and creates unrealistic expectations while minimizing the importance of brief, brightly burning loves that guide us through large and small life changes, help us negotiate the sharp turns of surprise upheavals, and stay afloat when everything else is sinking.

Some loves aren't meant to grow with you when the narrative of your life shifts. Some loves can't accommodate a geographical adjustment, changing interests, or seeking out new adventures. Are those loves less meaningful in that moment? No. Do we try to breathe life into things well past their expiration date? All the time.

Imagine if we were taught growing up that some relationships do last forever. That through luck and hard work and honesty and respect, some loves last a lifetime. But the majority of relationships are briefer than that. They have limited lifespans and can be just as valuable in those moments. Imagine if we were taught how to extricate ourselves from loves that had limits, if we were equipped with the conversational skills to discuss complex emotional situations with the same care and tenacity as learning to ride a bike or solve math equations. If we gave love, in all its forms, just the tiniest bit of work we could disavow ourselves of the ways that forever has stealthily, detrimentally infiltrated our lives.

When forever is positioned as a false equivalency to love — as is often the case in Céline Dion's songs and those of her contemporaries — the words, the infrastructure of this mythical promised land, is, on closer study, disturbing. Think about the type of lines we have all heard in countless songs: "I can't live without you" and "there's no living without you" and "I would die without you," and the list goes on. There is a very fine line between romantic and obsessive, and more often than not, the language of forever love is complicit in the insidious perpetuation of love as collateral, a person as property, and damaging co-dependency.

One could say I'm not a romantic, but that's not true. I'm deeply romantic — now. That's why love songs like this give me pause: at their darkest reading, they validate certain abuser dynamics, making it easier for predatory types to manipulate their targets. I've been on the receiving end of the "I would die without you" sentiment, and it may have been true for them, but it was also a way to make sure I wouldn't leave them, that I would stay no matter how toxic the situation. It prioritized their existence over mine and made me feel trapped, like it would be my fault if I did try to establish boundaries or leave. When a singer confesses they'd have no reason to live if their lover left, it's not just sad or depressing, it's also calculating and unfair. Another possible outcome of this dynamic — one's inability to handle rejection — is the very real and scary ways in which it has fuelled incel culture and the entitlement of (usually) straight white cisgender men who feel that women "owe" them sex, love, companionship, servitude, etc. At the very least, these types of songs infiltrate and exploit the innate vulnerabilities of love by perpetuating low self-esteem and romanticizing toxic relationships.

Of course, Dion would likely never see anything sinister or dark in the songs she chooses, or the songs that choose her. Céline Dion is in the business of love, and forever love is just one facet of the forty-carat diamond heart that is her life. There is a tremendous amount to enjoy and admire about Dion and her music. She's hugely talented. Her voice is incredible. She makes decent songs great, good songs soar, and terrible songs palatable. She's a shrewd business woman and exacting artist who had one goal and pursued it tenaciously. She worked to get what she wanted and sacrificed a normal childhood in pursuit of her dream. But she publicly and musically presents as though being in love is the be all and end all, and it's not. It's love and work ethic and talent and luck and compromise and illicit beginnings and sacrifice. Love, and especially her love story, is not a fairy tale in the Disney sense. Grimm's, though, now we're onto something.

Let's Talk About Love

This is one of the best-selling albums in history. Let that sink in for a second and then consider Christopher John Farley's review in *Time*: "the main problem with *Let's Talk About Love* is that Dion's sense of dynamics is only a trifle more refined than Saddam Hussein's sense of international protocol."[10] This record is seventy-five minutes long. It is overstuffed, overcooked, and overproduced — as wildly popular as it is wildly uneven, even by Dion's standards.

The album's lows outnumber the highs. It opens with the devotional eye-roller "The Reason," which credits her lover as the reason she gets out of bed and, you know, lives. These melodramatic declarations preclude one from establishing a strong

10 Christopher John Farley, "Music That Goes for the Rafters," *Time*, November 24, 1997, https://content.time.com/time/subscriber/article/0,33009,987422,00.html.

sense of self, and that level of tunnel vision is frankly irritating. On the surface, it's probably very sweet to toss out platitudes like the aforementioned, but in practice, it's deeply disturbing. Love shouldn't be a co-dependent, living nightmare. That's very *Fatal Attraction*, and look how that turned out.

"Immortality" is also a significant misstep, and not the last failed collaboration on this record. The Bee Gees pop up as special guests, which should be fun, but they only add more weight to the bloated, banal experience. The lyrics are a mess of contradictions and clichés that supposedly explore love, loss, and reincarnation but sound more like a messy translation missing key elements and phrases. And the arrangements actually sound insipid.

It's a different kind of disaster than the next track, "Treat Her Like a Lady," which pairs Dion with the song's original singer, reggae queen Diana King. The track has energy and heft, even if the lyrics offer up a questionable faux-feminism, and King is amazing, of course, but she can't save this song from its worst offense . . . Dion singing in a Jamaican patois. On first listen, the immediate conclusion is: THIS CANNOT BE REAL. It is insufferable. I hated it when Sting did it with the Police, I've hated it ever since then, and I hate it here. Appropriation is never the "tribute" white people think it is.

The next two songs, "Why Oh Why" and "Love Is on the Way," are also head-scratchers, from the vocal decisions to even being included on the record. Why is Dion's best-selling album to date chock full of crap? It's six songs before we even get to something memorable, substantial, and lasting. And this leads me back to some questions I've already raised: Would Dion even have half the career today in the age of singles? Would the phenomenon of streaming individual tracks power her further as people focused on her better songs, or would it reduce her impact, at least financially, because there are a lot of stinkers on her records and usually just two to four standouts. Does it even matter? Maybe not, but I think there's something to consider about the relative importance of song selection now more so than ever before.

"Tell Him," a duet with Barbra Streisand, is the turning point for the record, even if you are not a Streisand fan. I'm not, but even I can acknowledge the weird sort of thrill in hearing her and Dion join forces and take pleasure in Streisand's tacit welcoming of Dion into the ever-exclusive divas club. Lyrically, of course, the song is a cry for help: their flowery, overwrought back and forth is Dion singing as the younger woman afraid to tell a man how she feels, worried about appearing weak or hesitant or frail. Streisand is the older, wiser woman encouraging her protégé to, well, tell him. Every time somebody listens to this song, where womanhood and relationships are connected directly to fear and weakness, a dollar should be donated to a girls' rock camp.

From that song, why wouldn't you move directly into "Amar Haciendo el Amor," a Spanish-language cover with elegant guitar. I actually very much enjoy how Dion sequences this section of the record; placing this song right after her Streisand duet ensures more people give it a chance and shows her Spanish-language fans that she's prioritizing this track rather than burying it in that entirely forgettable first quarter.

It's almost surprising that it took Dion five English-language albums to cover the soft-rock ballad "When I Need You." It's totally surprising that she doesn't push it further, bigger, and bolder. It's weirdly restrained and the song itself is already a bit weak, so it could actually benefit from Dion and crew amping it up with some more bombast and soaring chorus work, as she does in the final third of the track.

"Miles to Go (Before I Sleep)" is a CanCon treasure. Written by Corey "Sunglasses at Night" Hart, the song challenges Dion to plumb new depths in her lower register. For a song based on a Robert Frost poem, the phrasing feels a bit clunky and it reads, again, like Dion is further defending her relationship with Angélil as her character lists all the things she'll do for the man she loves to prove her devotion and defend him to her last breath. Perhaps it's that fight that energizes her, the notion that this romance is forbidden; Dion literally calls out people who "sit in judgment" of the couple, but eventually her aggressive need to prove their love comes off as insecurity, the neediness of her delivery in opposition to the song's intention. Hart also produced the track, and there are a few stylistic elements — waiting room percussion and sleepy, Sunday-morning guitar riffs — that also hold the song back and keep it mid at best.

The naive notion that love is forever continues with "Us," another wholly devotional platitude that's bland as fuck and devoid of nuance. Dion continues to sound great — she brings some kind of life to even the dullest songs, but it's simply not enough to draw new fans to her material. When every lyric is a soap opera — melodramatic and over the top — there's an absence of keenly observed, relatable moments. Grand gestures and sky-high vows aren't universal experiences, and these dramatics negate Dion's ability to resonate on a wider scale. Obviously she was already a huge, international star and didn't need to be bigger, but judging by her work ethic and interviews, she always wanted to be the biggest star on the planet. If she had scaled back on the clichéd song choices and generalizations in her lyrics, even by ten percent, it's entirely possible she could have been without peer.

"Just a Little Bit of Love" is the sonic equivalent of a mirror ball of waking cocaine nightmares, but it's pretty fun just to have a different tempo to change things up. The beat is an aerobic workout's worth of repetition. Dion's extraordinary power is that even tossed-off songs like this feel like they have substance.

"My Heart Will Go On" is, of course, the centrepiece of the record. It's Dion's biggest hit and was the best-selling single of 1998. It's still one of the best-selling singles of all time. It's epic and weepy and emotionally manipulative, and yet I kind of love it. Actually, I totally love it, even though I also kind of hate it. That patented Dion hush lures you in, like a volcano puffing out gentle clouds of smoke, making people "ooh" and "ahh" over nature's miracle, and then it suddenly explodes and buries them all alive in molten lava.

Dion takes her time with "My Heart Will Go On." She gives it space to breathe before climbing into its upper rafters, and in its quieter moments, her voice takes on a youthful purr. For the first time, she sounds her age rather than reaching for middle age. There's power in Dion embracing her twenty-nine-year-old self, particularly since she has mostly sounded forty-five since she was twenty-one. This feels like a turning point for Dion, as if she's finally comfortable and confident in herself, her abilities, and her success. She inhabits this more youthful character beautifully, and there's so much nuance in her delivery; this is the Dion everybody had been waiting for.

"My Heart Will Go On" is such a high that it's impossible not to be disappointed in what follows. "Where Is the Love," another song by Hart, signals that we're in trouble with the hand-drum that sounds like it's supposed to double as a heartbeat, and then the tingly percussion confirms what we already suspect from the lyrical cliché about believing in dreams and spreading one's wings to fly. The song is terrible. "I Hate You Then Love You" is a duet with the late tenor Luciano Pavarotti, and the small mercy is that his and Dion's voices are much better suited than the collaboration he did that same year with the Spice Girls. But the lyrics occupy that unfortunate overlap of stupid and creepy, and the imagery they evoke as they trade verses is akin to torture porn or a sequel to *Misery*.

The album ends with the title track, "Let's Talk About Love," and continues Dion's tradition of title tracks being among the least successful songs on the album. Bryan Adams co-wrote the song, and a children's choir inexplicably pops up at one point, singing about how they're all the same because of one "true" emotion. Can you guess what that emotion is? Wait, wait, don't tell me.

Love?

Dion's notion of love is singular in its conception and execution. Her love songs are fantasies, escapes, dream-like paradises, or, for some, waking nightmares. No matter how much respect and admiration I have now for Dion and her accomplishments, no matter how many people worship at her heart-shaped altar, and no matter how talented she is or how hard she has worked, one core belief has stayed the same since I was fifteen years old, and I stand by it. From my heart to yours: if a Céline Dion record personifies your romantic relationship in any way, get out. Get out now.

***

Perhaps none of the artists in this book have had a more complicated, fraught, and, at times, fantastic decade than Céline Dion. In 2016, her husband, René Angélil, died following a long battle with throat cancer. Soon after, on the day of Angélil's funeral, Dion's brother Daniel also died from cancer. Six years later, on December 8, 2022, Dion publicly announced that, after experiencing ongoing health problems, she had been diagnosed with the rare neurological disorder stiff-person syndrome, a serious condition which causes muscle spasms and muscle rigidity.

Between these tragic and devastating life markers, Dion and her public persona experienced a wild and well-deserved uptick in popularity and social capital. It crept up on all of us, but by 2019, Céline Dion was everywhere and she was . . . cool!?! So much so, that Suzannah Showler deemed it the year of the "Célinaissance" in *The Walrus*,

> At fifty-one, Céline has arguably become Canada's greatest living icon. Parents love her, grandparents adore her, and now the younger generation is discovering that not only is she endlessly talented but also endlessly memeable. The internet swooned when she arrived at this year's Met gala looking like she'd been baptized in gold paint and sewn into a bodysuit slash bead curtain, a corona of singed peacock feathers growing straight out of her skull. Not long after, she sashayed through Paris Couture week and Twitter feeds like a living gif, serving such high-meets-low looks as a no-pants-no-problem

> scuba number with blazer, a gown that looked like sound waves rendered in mesh, and a replica of the honking *Titanic* jewel necklace worn over an "I Love Paris Hilton" T-shirt.[11]

It is fitting that fashion, a long-time passion and obsession for Dion, arguably played the biggest role in her reinvention. Finally Dion's high-fashion-meets-pop-culture-meta-memeability conveyed the star's fun, quirky, unapologetically weird side which had, at various points throughout her fame, manifested as awkward, cringe, and embarrassingly thirsty. Dion now seemed lighter, brighter, empowered, and, most importantly, in on the joke of her reputation as someone so overly earnest the only edges to her character were her high cheekbones. The force of Dion's feelings and her ability to convey every emotion simultaneously in a single note were too much for the irony-drenched '90s and the post-ironic aughts. By 2019, we were deep into a different world where feeling your honest feelings was what we all strived for: it was Dion's time to truly shine and be seen and celebrated in all of her glory.

In part, that was thanks to Dion finally finding the right partner to successfully establish her as a fashion icon. Famed stylist and self-described image architect Law Roach helped make Dion's haute couture dreams come true. It all started with a 2016 look that was instantly unforgettable: Dion in skinny jeans, large black sunglasses, and a very baggy black *Titanic* hoodie featuring Kate Winslet and Leonardo DiCaprio. Roach posted

---

11 Suzannah Showler, "Céline Dion Is Everywhere," *The Walrus*, August 28, 2019, https://thewalrus.ca/celine-dion-is-everywhere/.

the photo to his Instagram with the caption "Legendary," and he was right. The internet went wild and Dion seemed to relish her new role, turning out an endlessly innovative array of looks that were Roach specialties: glamorous, bold, playful, and audacious.

Dion discovered Roach through her youngest two children, twins Eddy and Nelson. They were big fans of the Disney show *K.C. Undercover* starring Zendaya, who had become a red carpet and high-fashion darling since she began working with Roach in 2011. Dion called Roach and the enormity of the moment took a while to sink in. "My first words were: Céline who?" Roach told *Vanity Fair* in 2017. "I don't think I had dreamt that big of a dream. That this legend, this woman who we've all grown up to her music, that's been around for 30 years, was calling me to work with me."[12]

Roach and Dion met in person in May 2016, just a few months after the deaths of her husband / manager and brother. The day after their meeting, she asked Roach to go with her to Paris for a month as both her stylist and to manage her tour wardrobe. According to the *Vanity Fair* article, he'd been by her side ever since. Roach told the magazine about the role fashion played in how Dion coped with her grief:

> She also credits me, and what we did, and the clothes, and the shoes, and the bags, and the jewelry, and couture week, and the shows, and all that to helping her through her grieving process. I'm sure her grieving process will never be over.

---

12 Erika Harwood, "How Céline Dion Became a Fashion Icon at 49," *Vanity Fair*, July 10, 2017, https://www.vanityfair.com/style/2017/07/celine-dion-law-roach-becoming-a-fashion-icon.

> She'll probably grieve her husband for the rest of her life because she was with him for so long. But she has said that what we did last year in Paris really helped her through that process. For me that's more than anything else. That's more than accolades, that's more than being interviewed by *Vanity Fair*, that is something that I'll take with me forever.[13]

Dion and Roach's sartorial collaboration helped transform Dion personally and publicly. A 2019 *Elle* profile, "Céline Dion Is Living Her Best Life," described the effect of one of Dion's most recent wardrobe wins: "Last July, a photo of her wearing a banana-yellow power suit and sunglasses went viral. In it, she defies gravity, perching on a windowsill, legs spread in a nearly 180-degree power stance. 'My Heart Will Go Off,' 'A New Slay Has Come,' 'It's All Coming Back to Memes,' declared Twitter. I would've given it a 'Big Dion Energy.' Whatever the caption, Céline projects the very now notion of women doing whatever the fuck they want."[14]

Dion was a badass fashion icon and feminist hero. Finally! It was a total 180 from the way most media talked about Dion in the 1990s during the first peaks of her fame. Hell, it was a total 180 from the way Dion talked about herself, unselfconsciously confessing her lack of agency and basic life skills, like checking into a hotel without Angélil. Twenty years later, Dion was a

13 Harwood, "How Céline Dion."

14 Katie Connor, "Celine Dion Is Living Her Best Life," *Elle*, May 1, 2019, https://www.elle.com/culture/celebrities/a27288491/celine-dion-elle-interview/.

different person. "Céline has no fear," Roach told *Vanity Fair*. "And when you have that type of energy, you have this attitude that we can do whatever we want and we don't care who likes it or dislikes it. Fashion is supposed to be polarizing. It has to be overwhelming."

In 2018, Dion used her newfound status as a fashionista to launch a line of gender-neutral clothing for kids. She talked about the importance of raising her own twins gender neutral: "If you're a boy you wear blue? Because you're a girl you wear pink? What is that? What people feel inside is not about a colour, it's how you feel. We have to give the children the opportunity to be who they are."[15] There was little backlash (as one might have expected given the divisiveness in politics at the time and now) against her progressive and inclusive foray into children's fashion; in fact, in 2019, Dion became the "global spokesperson" for L'Oréal Paris. Dion claimed the brand's "I'm Worth It" slogan was especially meaningful. "Telling other women that they, too, have self-worth, that they are strong, is obviously really important. You cannot limit yourself. My life started over at 50; I feel happy, I feel beautiful. I thought, 'I must have done something right for this to be happening.'"[16] For years, Dion told *Elle*, she'd let her vocal cords call the shots but not anymore. "I'm not saying that I don't care what people think of me, but I've reached a point in my life where I can let myself make my own decisions and choices. . . . Now I am discovering myself more and more.

15 Dan Wootton, "Second Wind Beneath My Wings: Celine Dion on the Younger Man in Her Life and Why She Feels Sexier Than Ever at 50," *Sun* (UK), January 29, 2019, https://www.thesun.co.uk/tvandshowbiz/8301240/celine-dion-hyde-park-concert-sexier/.

16 Connor, "Celine Dion."

I am a woman assuming her own destiny, full of energy and in love with life. It's never too late to start. At 51, I have the sense that I am at my pinnacle!"

The headlines and articles continued to exult Dion and her new role in pop culture, asking rhetorical questions like "What did we do to deserve Céline Dion?" and praising the live, laugh, love vibe that was underscoring her every move. The cheese factor that had long been associated with Dion's "brand" could be hokey and corny, but it could also be authentic and cool, and the culture was finally far enough along — at least when it came to Dion — that the multiplicity of her truths could co-exist. She told *The Sun*, "I feel that now I have a voice, which is kinda weird as that's what I've been doing all my life — using my voice, but in singing and performing. But I use my voice as well for things that I choose I want to do and things that I say to my team I don't want to do. I feel that I am grown up enough to say, 'I think I would rather do this than that.' I'm not playing 50. I'm not playing that, 'I'm the boss now.' I don't want to do that. I don't necessarily want to be the boss. I just want to be the best of me and be surrounded — like my husband always surrounded me with — the best people."[17]

But the "Célinaissance" wasn't just about her new fashion icon status, or that she was impressing people with the ways in which she seemed to be surviving the loss of her husband/manager. It was also reflected in the way that critics wrote about Dion's 2019 album, *Courage*. In another 180 from the '90s, the reviews were largely positive, praising Dion's vitality and experimental nature with the record's forays into

17 Wootton, "Second Wind."

dance-pop and EDM alongside her trademark power ballads and urgent, emotional love songs. *Billboard*, *Slate*, and *Idolator* called *Courage* one of the best albums of the year. Even a mixed review from *Variety* ended with this begrudging endorsement: "At least half of the album is fantastic. But don't let her make a habit out of this."[18]

Three years later, there were hints that something was going on with Dion behind the scenes. On June 16, 2022, Roach posted a picture of Dion boarding a plane and captioned it: "She changed my life….. I will forever be grateful! Love you @celinedion."[19] Six months later, Dion took to her Instagram page and posted a video in which she announced the cancellation of her world tour and her stiff-person syndrome diagnosis. In the video, she described how the condition was affecting every aspect of her daily life: "Sometimes causing difficulties when I walk and not allowing me to use my vocal cords to sing the way I'm used to. It hurts me to tell you this today."[20] The spasms, which can be severe enough to cause falls, can be triggered by everything from bright lights to sudden loud sounds to intense cold. Five months later, in May 2023, Dion's team announced the further cancellation of her world tour through 2023 and 2024. Dion tweeted: "I'm so sorry to disappoint all of you once again . . . and even though it breaks my heart,

---

18 A.D. Amorosi, "Album Review: Celine Dion's 'Courage,'" *Variety*, November 15, 2019, https://variety.com/2019/music/reviews/celine-dion-courage-album-review-1203406094/.

19 Law Roach (@luxurylaw), "She changed my life . . ." Instagram, June 18, 2022, https://www.instagram.com/p/Ce-HR6pLaJS/?img_index=1.

20 Céline Dion (@celinedion), "I've been dealing with problems with my health for a long time . . ." Instagram, December 8, 2022, https://www.instagram.com/p/Cl5xJY1AjAO/.

it's best that we cancel everything until I'm really ready to be back on stage . . . I'm not giving up . . . and I can't wait to see you again!"[21] After largely staying out of the spotlight for more than a year to focus on her illness, Dion surprised the audience and her fans when she presented at the 2024 Grammy Awards. Styled by Roach in a divine floor-length, fawn-coloured, mohair Valentino coat over a pale pink silk gown, Dion was greeted by a standing ovation when she appeared on stage to award the winner of the evening's biggest honour, record of the year. But after announcing Taylor Swift as the winner, Swift came up on stage and failed to acknowledge Dion in any meaningful way. The internet and media went wild, calling out Swift for "snubbing" Dion on the night of her triumphant return to public life.

This outpouring of love for Dion — and the protective tone of the brief backlash towards Swift for not giving Dion her flowers — is, honestly, a delight to witness. The pop culture narrative around Dion has course-corrected significantly in the last decade, celebrating her on her own terms, and I'm here for the "Célinaissance." Writing the first iteration of this book helped rewrite my relationship to Dion, but the last decade has allowed that appreciation to grow into something like love. I'm not the only one. The media's evolving position on Dion is most evident in the reviews that followed the release of the 2023 film *Love Again*, in which Dion was lauded frequently as the best part of the movie (*The Guardian*'s headline: "Céline Dion Is

---

21 "Celine Dion Cancels 2023–24 Shows over Health Condition," *Al-Jazeera*, May 26, 2023, https://www.aljazeera.com/news/2023/5/26/celine-dion-cancels-2023-24-shows-over-health-condition.

the High Note of Sappy Romcom").[22] The film, made in 2020 largely during Covid, is a remake of a 2016 German film, *SMS für Dich*, which was based on a 2009 novel of the same name. In *Love Again*, a woman texts her dead fiancé's number only to discover, eventually, that the number now belongs to a man who is dealing with similar heartbreak while writing a profile of Dion. Not only does Dion appear as herself in the film, she also recorded the titular theme song and four more songs for the soundtrack. In it, she gets to effusively expound on a subject in which she has made herself the go-to expert: love. She gets to be funny, ferocious, wise, and tender, and she also gets to give some real talk about heartbreak.

I am in no way surprised that this is the film Dion signed on for given the open and honest ways she's talked about coping with the loss of her husband/manager. This detail from the 2019 *Walrus* essay reads like satire, and yet I believe it wholly, and in part I understand it. When I read it the first time, I was in an especially vulnerable state. It is macabre and weird and she is an extremely rich person, but it's also heartbreakingly real and relatable. I was both chilled by it and so moved that I burst into tears and cried for at least five minutes. "The pair had a secret handshake, dancing their fingers at each other like baseball coaches signalling a play. Before a show, she would lay the fingers of her right hand on his left and hold them there until they both felt it: connection. Now she does it before every show with an effigy — a literal replica of Angélil's hand, cast in bronze."[23]

22 Adrian Horton, "Love Again Review — Céline Dion Is the High Note of Sappy Romcom," *Guardian*, May 5, 2023, https://www.theguardian.com/film/2023/may/05/love-again-review-celine-dion-priyanka-chopra-jonas.

23 Showler, "Céline Dion."

Whew. That is the Dion I've always known and have grown to love. I understand devastating loss and holding on to comfort any way that you can. I appreciate her emotional rawness, the way she wears her feelings so nakedly and without any sense of shame or self-protection. All the things that I used to think she must be exaggerating to perform perpetual princess cosplay, all the things I used to hold against her, I don't anymore. Vulnerability is not weakness, and neither is love. Misogyny and sexism, of course, tell us otherwise, but those jerks don't know shit. Dion's strength, her gift to all of us, has been that she has always known the power of love, literally and lyrically, and she's always been unapologetically vulnerable, even when the rest of the world viciously mocked her for it. Dion's diagnosis is not the future she or her loved ones or her fans envisioned, and it sucks. If anybody can get through this, it's Céline Dion. She does not give up. Her ambition is as big as her love, and her heart, music, and cultural impact will absolutely go on.

SHANIA TWAIN

Bad Feelings, Bare Midriffs, and Breaking Ground

It's been more than three decades since Shania Twain's self-titled debut was released. In the space of just five years, from 1993 to 1997, Twain hit the country music industry like a grenade. She made women-centric pop crossovers a modern country staple (you're welcome, the Chicks and Taylor Swift) and her third album, *Come on Over*, is one of the biggest and best-selling country albums of all time.

But for me, at least, her legacy is a complicated one. As a teenager, I couldn't stand Twain. I vehemently objected to her brand of coy, sexy country-pop that I felt pushed women's equality back ten or fifteen years. I wrote her off as a construct of male fantasy: a girl who could ride a horse while showing off a perfectly sculpted bare midriff by day and slip into some sort of cleavage-baring cocktail dress at night, the emphasis always on her sex appeal first, relatability second, and talent third.

I didn't give Twain the credit she deserved. I couldn't see her success as giving value to women. But it did. And it does. I didn't notice or understand her skilful manipulation of the surface to push her subversive, secret agenda — an agenda that would change country music, for a little while at least, and give rise to a new generation of women writing their own material. Because I didn't care about her songs and dismissed her music, I assumed Twain was masking an absence of talent with an abundance of flesh. But on all of her albums, Twain asserted what she wanted as a woman, or at least what her characters wanted. She didn't do it in service of the male gaze but in service of herself. Throughout her career, Twain asserted over and over that a woman's voice was just as important as a man's, and she used hers to reiterate that point. But I was too busy focusing on the damned crop tops to bother listening. It's time to make amends.

Twain was born Eilleen Regina Edwards in 1965, and she learned early on that if she wanted a better life, she would need to be its architect. She wrote her own accounts of growing up in Timmins, Ontario, and the challenging environment in which she was raised: extreme poverty, malnourishment, and parents who were chronically underemployed. Twain started singing in bars for money when she was just eight years old, waiting until after midnight when they'd stopped serving alcohol. Her mother and her adoptive father sometimes fought violently, and there were attempts by her mother to leave, though the separations never lasted. Twain started writing songs when she was ten years old and slowly built a name for herself as an emerging singer-songwriter, playing in cover bands and performing her own material. In 1987, Twain attempted to break into pop and rock during a short stint in Nashville but was forced to return home to raise her younger siblings after her parents were killed in a car accident.

By 1993, Twain had adopted the stage name Shania, in and of itself a controversy. At first she claimed it was an Ojibwe word and a salute to her heritage, though it was her adoptive father who was actually Ojibwe. Later, she claimed she was part Cree thanks to her biological father. Neither language claims the word "Shania." What is clear amid this cultural confusion and probable appropriation, however, is that Twain has always been the author of her own identity and remade herself to her own specifications, no one else's.

In that same year, she put together a demo that would become her self-titled debut. There are a few great spots on the record, including the instant country classic "Dance with the One That Brought You." A trio of back-to-back tracks on the last half established Twain's perspective on a country staple: heartbreak. "There Goes the Neighborhood" details breakups in Anytown, U.S.A., and the self-destruction that takes place when relationships go bust, homes and hearts falling apart with equal force. "Forget Me" is a nice middle finger to an ex and a fairly uptempo number considering the lover-scorned material was typically fodder for something more "woe is me" and downtempo. "When He Leaves You" is perhaps the most interesting effort, as it positions a fragile solidarity between a put-upon wife and a mistress who doesn't know that he won't leave the Mrs. It's a perfectly sorrowful country number that rejects the cats-with-claws stereotype of women fighting over the same loser.

The record's best offering, "God Ain't Gonna Getcha for That," showcases the fact that Twain was capable of far more than recording other people's songs. The song is her sole writing credit on her debut (it's for co-writing), and it's a knockout that elevates the album in every way. It's energetic, upbeat, and catchy as hell, and it hints at the country-pop she was ready to unleash on the world. It's also a great starting point for those needing proof of Twain's voice as a writer and of her women empowerment agenda. The song itself advocates sexual agency and rejects faith-based morality, a double no-no in country music in 1993. The song is Twain's warning flare to the country music stalwarts that change is coming in the form of women-centred pop crossovers.

Twain's second record was the game changer, and it flowed out of the partnership, both creative and romantic, that developed between her and producer Robert "Mutt" Lange. Lange came from a rock and soft-rock background, producing and writing or co-writing tracks for artists such as AC/DC, Heart, and Def Leppard. He reached out after hearing some of the tracks on Twain's debut and offered to write and produce a few songs for her next record. Lange had Americana dreams, she had pop ones, and their subsequent love story moved at the speed of wild horses. They talked over the phone every day for weeks, met in June 1993, started writing together, and were married before the end of the year.

Together the couple co-wrote or wrote all the songs on Twain's 1995 record, *The Woman in Me*. It was an interesting title that allowed for different interpretations, from the reflexive, sexist eye-rolling about "chick music" to the belief in a romance novel's worth of melodrama. Some regarded it as the push-pull between a woman's identity and agency. It could be read matter-of-factly or entrenched in subtext. Perhaps the title reflected a powerful person at war with her own hypersexualized persona, her everyday sexuality, and her integrity as an artist; someone who vacillates between finding power within versus finding power in the love of a man. It's a rich title that either indulges armchair psychology, provokes snap judgment dismissals, or inspires a call to action and feminine solidarity.

The record opens with "Home Ain't Where His Heart Is (Anymore)," a good song that's more a polished sad ballad (very Lange-esque) than a crossover contender. It's indicative of Twain's new direction, and there's at least one key shift that proves inspired. There's also a wailing guitar lick that's straight out of a Bryan Adams song, which isn't a huge surprise given that Lange produced Adams's *Waking Up the Neighbours* in 1991.

"Any Man of Mine" is definitely a throwback to Johnny Cash and June Carter Cash, and it's the sound of fun and it's also overflowing with bullshit gender clichés. It reminds me why I disliked Twain so much originally, and the choreographed dance — as if trying to make this the new "Achy Breaky Heart" — feels unnecessary. Conversely, "Whose Bed Have Your Boots Been Under?" is an instant country classic, as is the message of calling an errant lover to task for cheating. Frankly, it's nice to have an upbeat song wherein the scorned party isn't mournful and broken-hearted but sassy, matter-of-fact, and moving on.

"(If You're Not in It for Love) I'm Outta Here" prioritizes a woman's wants over a man's, and it's glorious. When Twain sings this song, written from a woman's point of view, she's advocating that a woman's needs should never take a backseat to a man's. It's also one of Twain's first songs to feature a remix version that substantially strips away the country twang and amps up the pop-rock. Releasing dual versions of her songs to both country and pop radio was a brilliant move that she would repeat with the majority of her singles, ensuring nary an ear could escape Twain's reach.

"The Woman in Me (Needs the Man in You)" represents everything I despised about Twain. It feels like yet another song reducing women to half creatures who need men to be whole. I have not come around on this song. On top of the song having a sexist conceit, the majority of the lyrics seem to prioritize the rhyme scheme over saying anything coherent. Twain sings about not always being strong like a rock and that sometimes she's wrong but she wins when she chooses, and I'm still trying to figure out what in the ever-loving fuck that even means. That we're still bashing ourselves over the heads with the same old idea that it's novel for a strong woman to also enjoy and value the loving arms of a partner? Oh, shoot. And with that I actually sort of talked myself into seeing why Twain wrote it, because sadly that concept was still novel back then. Hell, it's novel now for a lot of people.

The next two songs, "Is There Life after Love?" and "If It Don't Take Two," failed to make the cut as singles, and it's easy to identify why: both are lyrically mediocre, and while drastically different musically, they each fall flat in similar ways. But what follows is interesting. Apart from their joint compositions, Lange and Twain each contributed a solo track to the record. Lange's offering, "You Win My Love," is essentially a love letter to the NASCAR set. Lyrically, it's almost embarrassingly stereotypically masculine with its non-stop car and driving metaphors, but musically, it offers interesting instrumentation — fiddle and string arrangements balance out the honky-tonk of the guitar — and its sound is different enough from the rest of the album that it illuminates Lange's role.

"Raining on Our Love" is a mournful little breakup ballad, but the next song, "Leaving Is the Only Way Out," demands the most attention. It's Twain's solo tune, and it recalls the great Patsy Cline. It's one of the best tracks on the record. There's a genuine vintage country gem hidden under all that production — I would love to hear a version that's just Twain and the lap steel. It's lyrically heartfelt and the chorus is a compelling wake-up call that if your partner thrives on your pain, leaving is the only option.

The record ends on a weird high and low: "No One Needs to Know," which also found a home on the *Twister* soundtrack, is a fun, sweet little ditty. It initially also ruffled my feminist feathers, but I've since calmed down. The song is about the heady fantasies that can accompany falling in love, looking into the future, and making plans for the church, the dress, and the kids that follow (down to their names). Some women secretly plan to marry their partners well before it's advisable. So do some men. The divorce rate is pretty high, so really do marriage fantasies even matter? "God Bless the Child" is a clunker, though, even if the intentions were good, particularly because it reinforces some pretty broad stereotypes about "at-risk" kids before moving into the requisite gospel flourishes that characterized global relief songs. A strange capper on an album that otherwise is all about romantic love and all its various states.

***

Twain's decision not to tour in support of *The Woman in Me* gave her detractors plenty of ammunition in their argument that she was a studio concoction with no real ability to perform or sing live. Twain refuted this repeatedly, and in a 1997 *Billboard* interview, she pointed out her long history as a road warrior.

> I was on the road in my parents' car playing clubs from a very early age. Then I was in a van with all the guys and the equipment. I toured all the way up to the end of my first album. In my opinion, I've paid my dues as far as touring is concerned. I was able to prove that you can sell records through radio and television just on the basis of the music. You don't have to have all the hoopla. Sometimes the industry underestimates the fans. There are only a few women who have sold what I have sold in North America. The other two are Céline Dion and Alanis Morissette, and the only one who achieved those sales without touring was me. They probably could have as well, because their albums were excellent. But now I can add the touring element.[1]

Between 1995 and 1997, there was also a lot of ink spilled debating Twain's merit as an artist and value as a singer: Talentless sex strumpet? Pin-up pop wannabe? Was she saving country or condemning it? Was she a role model or the poster girl for entrenched patriarchy?

---

1 Chet Flippo, "Twain Branches Out on Sophomore Set," *Billboard*, October 18, 1997.

And then *Come on Over* arrived. Its first track, "Man! I Feel Like a Woman!," was a huge fuck you to the critics and haters. The lyrics are infuriating, I wrote in 2015, but I see now how they're also fun, trolling, and subversive. She plays with gendered expectations and stereotypes of femininity — short skirts, colouring her hair, having fun — they're a send-up of the persona for which Twain was being constantly condemned. She centres the conversation on her own body, and in making it about veneer and surface, she's almost provoking the naysayers.

It seems like mindless stuff, and yet there was a lot of intention behind what she and Lange were both doing with this persona they constructed. Twain was a strong woman with a lot of agency who was frequently asserting that agency in public, but because she is also beautiful and seemingly enjoyed showing off her body, she wasn't perceived as a feminist threat, even if what she was doing was, in fact, deeply feminist, including exercising her prerogative to look and sound any way she wanted. It was the moral majority and hardcore feminists who condemned Twain most loudly, and that's what gave me pause for thought in recontextualizing Twain's legacy and revisiting my assessment of her and her work. As a feminist, my views about Twain — her beauty, her songs, and how I judged her as being largely in service of the male gaze — were dangerously rubbing up against those of my natural enemies: moral purists and religious zealots. Policing a woman's body is anti-feminist; what was I doing? It was a huge realization, and it forced me to step back and reassess what was really driving my objections. The answer had nothing to do with sex or a sexy image. Rather, it was all about stupid lyrics and my interpretation of them as vapid, man-crazy, reinforcing gendered stereotypes, etc.

Conflating my internalized misogyny and equating that with my then less inclusive feminism was a second-wave trap that I fell into.

"I'm Holdin' on to Love (To Save My Life)" is power-pop country with lots of momentum. It's overproduced and shiny; it's also compelling and catchy with neat beats in the chorus. The little guitar twang break is fun, even if the drums feel a bit stale.

"Love Gets Me Every Time" is interesting, since Twain really does continue to present two distinct but connected sides: a woman who defines herself by her love, and a woman attempting to assert her sense of self. It's a better track than what follows: "Don't Be Stupid (You Know I Love You)" is a line-dancing, electro-funk fiddle jam, and it's another dual personality song where the character is frustrated with her jealous lover but also perpetuates the cliché of being a woman who can't live without said man. It's another track that features multiple treatments and releases, and the country version is definitely superior to the club thumper track.

"From This Moment On" was (and sometimes is) the ultimate wedding song, particularly in its original incarnation as a duet with Bryan White. While Twain's vocals are fine, White's scratch at the ears. The solo version quickly eclipsed the duet version in popularity, and the addition of Spanish-style guitar was a wise choice.

The next three songs feel like they could have been cut to make the record thirteen tracks instead of sixteen. But "Come on Over" received a calypso treatment and went on to win a Grammy, so what do I know about the world? "When" is a strange tune in that Twain's voice sounds purposefully whiny, and the lyrics use real-life painful things (like wishing that John Lennon was alive) in trite ways that border on exploitative or heartless. "Whatever You Do! Don't!" is a crime of superfluous punctuation. The song's sole redeeming factor: a strong fiddle presence.

"If You Wanna Touch Her, Ask!" is one of the few country songs to address consent. Consider that this is still a topic of much debate, discussion, and contention (which is bullshit, of course) and then give Twain a standing O because it's unlikely that any label or studio wanted this on the tracklist. It has a powerful message that is simple, strong, and subtle.

"You're Still the One" is a sweet song that felt like a public declaration that Twain and Lange's love was the real thing, and not, as was constantly suggested by a variety of sexist, misogynist types, a case of Twain using him to get ahead. It's discouraging that people still believe Dion and Twain were fronts for their Svengalis. After all, nobody attributes Ozzy Osbourne's musical prowess or success to Sharon Osborne, or assumes that he's just a puppet dancing on her strings, but those assumptions still shape conversations about Dion and Twain. It's sexist and demeaning, and it's also an affront to our collective intelligence, equivalent to people still believing that the Earth is flat or that vaccines are bad or that there's no such thing as evolution. There's a relatively simple fix at hand: thorough research from credible sources about both of their careers and critical thinking, the BFFs of changing narratives and informed opinions. "You're Still the One" was a love letter but it was also Twain's attempt at proving her relationship was an actual partnership, too.

"Honey, I'm Home" was two steps forward, one step back. It offers a nice gender flip in that the central figure, a woman, is the breadwinner who's coming home to her house husband.

However, there's continued lyrical emphasis on what constitutes "women's problems."

"That Don't Impress Me Much" was another huge single for Twain and was possibly the least country track on the album. Despite the somewhat facile, simple lyrics, it was another gender flip of a song, putting Twain in the position of power to reject entitled men who think they're special. It's kind of refreshing to hear a song from a woman's point of view that's purely about putting "those guys" in their place and reinforcing a woman's agency.

"Black Eyes, Blue Tears" is another bold bit of social commentary. The song's protagonist decides to leave an abusive relationship. Considering what Twain witnessed between her parents while she grew up, it's easy to understand why she wrote this. The treatment is pretty pop-heavy, and there are a lot of quick-fix lyrics considering it's a song about domestic abuse, but it's an important message to come from someone of Twain's influence and stature. It's also an interesting precursor to the Chicks' rollicking "Goodbye Earl." Released three years later, in 2000, the earworm about disappearing a violent spouse pushed the cultural narrative further towards its *Fried Green Tomatoes* conclusion.

The open heartbreak of "Black Eyes, Blue Tears" is a total shift in direction from the Disney-esque pop ballad "I Won't Leave You Lonely," which sounds like a filler number that should be sung by an alligator with a quasi-racist Cajun accent and a bunch of fireflies lighting up the night during a will-they-or-won't-they rom-com montage.

"Rock This Country!" is another tick in the column for unnecessary punctuation, and the attempt at an all-American anthem feels like pandering. Does that really matter, though, to

Twain's American fans? No, if anything, it plays like a nice tribute to the country that embraced her wholeheartedly, and it's the most successful fusion of rock and country on the record, even if it's repetitive and by the numbers.

To provide some context as to how ridiculously successful this record was, the album came out in 1997 and they were still releasing singles in 1999, such as its final track, "You've Got a Way." It's sweet, sappy, slow, and romantic. Twain also released a remix that featured in the Hugh Grant/Julia Roberts romantic comedy *Notting Hill*, pushing it higher up the charts and broadening its reach.

In the space of five years, Twain released three records, each more successful than the next. In fact, on March 12, 2015, Guinness World Records certified *Come on Over* as the best-selling solo record by a female solo artist with 40 million copies sold.[2] Still, many conversations about Twain and her success go one of two ways: she had to get naked to get on the radio, and/or she only married her husband for his music connections and to make her famous. On May 27, 2008, thirteen long years after Twain first worked with Lange on *The Woman in Me*, the *Globe and Mail* ran a piece with the headline "How Did Shania's Svengali Lose the One He Brung?" The online *Canadian Encyclopedia* entry on Twain, which was last updated October 17, 2022, still refers to Lange as a Svengali. These are things I thought when I was fifteen, a lifetime ago, and I can say with absolute love for my teenaged self: I was short-sighted and wrong.

---

2 Guinness World Records, "Biggest-selling studio album by a female solo artist," March 12, 2015, https://www.guinnessworldrecords.com/world-records/383776-biggest-selling-studio-album-by-a-female-solo-artist.

***

It's been a long road getting to a place where I can appreciate Twain. There are still people who don't feel that Twain and Dion have a right to share space with Morissette and McLachlan — not as peers, Canadian success stories, international icons, or musicians. Despite their inarguable success and influence, Twain and Dion were somehow national embarrassments for "serious" music fans, constructs of their husbands, puppets devoted to selling sex (or sexlessness) and pop mediocrity, shameless in their peddling of popular but harmful stereotypes about women for fame and profit.

Despite the fact that Twain co-wrote or wrote her most successful albums, I've seen it posited that Lange and Twain were involved in some kind of country-pop *Pygmalion* wherein he was the brains and she was the voice and body. It's sexist and gross, and I'm mad at myself that I bought into that notion as a teenager without questioning who was perpetuating it and who benefitted from it. If anything, there's reasonable evidence that Lange hitched a ride on Twain's coattails. Look back at Twain's debut album and her first co-writing credit, "God Ain't Gonna Getcha for That," and it's easy to see the foundation was already there for *The Woman in Me*, *Come on Over*, and *Up!* Twain's vision was country-pop and her songwriter's voice already had clarity and direction.

Lange's most prominent relationship was with Bryan Adams, with whom he won a Grammy in 1991 for "(Everything I Do) I Do It for You." The majority of Lange's other Grammys came from his work with Twain, and frankly, his work with Adams was uneven at best. There were some hugely commercial highs, like "Everything I Do," but there were also some stunning missteps that resulted in a lot of blows to Adams's reputation and musical credibility. 1996's *18 til I Die* received one and a half stars out of four from *USA Today*'s reviewer who implored Adams to "grow up already."[3]

It's not possible to parse Lange's contributions from Twain's when they share co-writing credits, but by focusing on the two tracks from *The Woman in Me* that feature solo credits for each of them, it's easy to see that Twain's song is three Stetsons taller than his. But even if one has successfully argued that no, Twain did not fuck her way to the top of the charts, there's another equally cruel way to dismiss her success and devalue her contributions to pop culture: *She's all bare midriffs and sexy videos. She's all boobs and bare skin, no substance. She's a disgrace to real women who don't need to show skin to get ahead. She's anti-feminist.*

That could have been my diary entry thirty years ago, and I hate that about myself, but it's time to come clean. I was a teenaged slut-shamer.

Let's face it: if you watched all of Twain's music videos back to back and drank every time you saw her abs, you'd be dead by the end of the playlist. As a teenager, I felt more familiar with Twain's body than my own. Because everything she wore and sang seemed to be in service of men, I figured that she was basically selling her body to sell her records and the by-product

3 Edna Gunderson, "Bryan Adams Regresses; Dylan Is Redone — with Strings," *USA Today*, July 2, 1996.

of that was contributing to the objectification of women and reinforcing the patriarchy. At best I was precocious. At worst I was enormously judgmental.

I had a pretty good grip on what my politics were and a firm grasp on my basic beliefs even as a teenager: pro-equality, pro-choice, and pro-smart, arty weirdos; anti-machismo, anti-violence, and anti-unquestioning acquiescence. In tenth grade, I went to my first Take Back the Night march by myself. Of course I loved Alanis Morissette and Sarah McLachlan, and of course I despised Shania Twain and Céline Dion. I viewed Twain and Dion as the antithesis of everything I valued, and I was quick to dismiss not only their music but also their fans, a few of whom were among my closest friends.

These days I try to be conscientious of the fact that I don't need to shit on one thing to illustrate why I love a different thing. It's ugly to be that kind of snob, but I did it a lot back then. I probably still do, since I find it hard to feign enthusiasm for things I strongly dislike or don't care about. I am a critic; I can sometimes be quite harsh and resolute in my assessment of a person's or thing's shortcomings or flaws, but it's just my opinion and people need only take me as seriously as they want to, so no big deal. However, being a critic is something I've grown into, and I've tried to be critical of myself and my own views as well. Dismantling my thoughts on Twain and my own ill-informed biases is part of that process.

I was hard on Twain because I believed her fame was equal only to her pin-up appeal. It felt like she was being rewarded for going along with the patriarchal charade that women need to be perceived as twice as sexy as they are talented to make it. At fifteen, I was deeply invested in my role as a feminist gatekeeper.

But finding ways to exclude and/or deny women their own experiences and opinions resembles, at worst, misogyny, and at best, the plot of *Mean Girls* or *Heathers*.

Eventually I would figure out that these exhausting and rigid feminist rules were kind of crap, and that those rules came at the expense of the liberation, inspiration, and equality that had always made me believe feminism was for me. I hid behind feminism to justify my contempt, but I also used feminism to come to terms with those feelings and re-educate myself. It's fully possible to reject and challenge perceived clichés and stereotyping in Twain's songs without bringing her appearance into it, but I had conflated all of it. I ignored the ground she was breaking, and I only saw what I wanted: shattered progress in service to her success.

As much as I shouted about women being strong individuals who could dress, say, do, and fuck however and whatever they wanted, I also erred on the side of being secretly conservative. To my teenage self, Twain in her crop tops lacked the authenticity of, say, Sarah McLachlan, because Twain had to show skin to get famous. She sold her body, whereas McLachlan sold her art. That was bullshit and I was a hypocrite and here's why: Twain can dress however she wants, in whatever way makes her feel good, without being judged by self-righteous gatekeepers and without being degraded for what she wears or what she does not wear. Also, McLachlan wasn't exactly a never-nude in her music videos and in magazines. It was just that Twain's body was more likely to be idealized, fetishized, and objectified, and that was the real problem. McLachlan's more "normal" body didn't satisfy the male gaze in the same way, but Twain wasn't necessarily looking to satisfy anyone's gaze but her own. Or, even if she was, why wasn't my anger directed at the male gaze? Probably because, when I was fifteen, I hadn't quite heard of that yet, even though it absolutely ruled my life and informed so much of my pop culture.

Reducing Twain to just a body and reducing her significant triumphs to her sex appeal are hugely unfair to her. It perpetuates a smug misogyny that tacitly permits removing talent from the equation when calculating a woman's level of success, thereby devaluing that success and making it not something she earned, but something she happened upon or got by exploitation. *If she can exploit her body, why shouldn't I?* the world bitterly asks, and so numerous narratives spin out from there, stereotypes are reinforced, attitudes and actions reaffirmed.

So who am I to strip Twain of agency over her career, wardrobe, and identity? I despise the fact that I've been complicit in these things because it's the opposite of the world in which I want to live. The mentality that a woman deserves less respect because she's dressed a certain way is slippery, shitty justification for a variety of terrible actions and attitudes that fuck up the world, maintain patriarchy, and perpetuate rape culture. I want a world that's safe for all women. When one perpetuates the notion that a woman deserves less respect or less humanity because of what she wears or what she doesn't wear, all women lose. Policing a woman's body is asserting ownership over it, and that's about as far from equality as you can get.

I don't believe Twain is un-feminist; if anything, I'd argue that she's a modern feminist. She figured out how to succeed and drive her own agenda in a male-dominated industry. She created the crossover country-pop genre. She wrote and co-wrote her own material, adding women-penned material to the country and pop canons. Twain gamed the system and made it work for her, and at the height of her success, she said, "Fuck it," and dropped out of sight, holing up in Switzerland and living a quiet life of her own making. If a man had achieved even half of the success that Twain had achieved in the space of ten years, he would be lauded, feted, and made a music legend. He would not have an asterisk beside his name, real or imagined, qualifying every achievement and tainting every triumph.

There's nothing to be gained by minimizing or erasing a woman's achievements based solely on what she wears or doesn't wear. It's possible to critique Twain and her actions without summarily dismissing her because of the bare midriffs. Critique Twain instead by focusing on her occasional weakness for trite lyrics, appropriation of an Indigenous identity, or perpetuation of tired gender clichés. But none of these things do as much damage to her legacy as those damned bare midriffs because as much as we may live in a patriarchy that has defined what it means to be sexy, that same patriarchy condemns women who decide to be sexy on their own terms, women like Anna Nicole Smith, Britney Spears, or Pamela Anderson (all of whom have had reputational resurrections in recent years to make up for the misogynistic ways they were discussed in the '90s). And when those half-naked pop stars are slut-shamed and their talent and success are overlooked and disqualified by the ever-present pearl-clutchers of the world, well then, the patriarchy, and not the women, wins.

If Dion's past decade has been complicated, fraught, and fantastic, Twain's has been an exercise in survival, reclamation, vindication, and revitalization. She got the messy gossip of her divorce from her husband and musical partner, Mutt Lange, out of the way with her 2011 memoir, *From This Moment On*, and dished about her relatively quick second marriage to Frédéric Thiébaud, the ex-husband of her former best friend, Marie-Anne Thiébaud, whose affair with Lange sparked his and Twain's 2008 separation. In the book, Twain also wrote candidly and with heartbreaking clarity about the poverty and abusive environment in which she was raised. The memoir was Twain's first major artistic expression that was hers alone, and it both cleared the air and reintroduced her to the world on her own terms, in her own voice. It was the first time that her audience got to meet the "real" Shania Twain, and it paved the way for Twain to truly get to know herself, too.

"I think I've remained very detached from my life to this point, almost as though it was a different person, every phase I went through," Twain told *Nightline* in 2011. "So I've reconnected and said no, this is actually who I am. I'm neither embarrassed of who I am, where I come from, what I've experienced — I'm not ashamed of it."[4]

In the book, Twain also revealed that her hiatus from music and touring wasn't just about raising her child or needing time off after three blockbuster albums. She had also been coping with vocal cord problems since 2004 and was ultimately diagnosed with dysphonia. She documented part of her vocal rehabilitation in the six-part 2011 docuseries *Why Not? With Shania Twain*

4 ABC News, "Shania Twain Opens Up about Her Difficult Childhood, Heart-Wrenching Divorce and Finding Love Again," *Nightline*, May 4, 2011, https://abcnews.go.com/Entertainment/shania-twain-opens-difficult-childhood-heart-wrenching-divorce/story?id=13529925.

on Oprah Winfrey's OWN. In 2014, she resumed performing again, first with a Las Vegas residency and then a world tour, both of which set the stage for Twain's comeback album — her first since 2002's *Up!* and her first without Lange since her 1993 debut — 2017's *Now*.

This was the record that had critics, fans, and haters waiting to see who, if anybody, had been right about Lange's presumed influence and control on Twain's music or if she was as much an equal partner behind the scenes as was indicated in the songwriting credits. It wasn't enough that she was the superstar propping up country music as the genre's best-selling artist and also out onstage performing dynamic, sold-out shows whilst being scrutinized, criticized, and objectified in a massive public spotlight. *Now* was never going to be perfect, not with that comeback pressure on Twain and her collaborators, but it had to be good enough to silence the naysayers and reintroduce Twain to the world, reaffirming her as an agent of her own change and the creator of her own sound and image. She wrote every song and co-produced every track, which was a shift from how she worked with Lange. "I was just a sounding board for Mutt when he was ready for me whereas here, I was more of a director," Twain told the *New York Times*.[5]

Now's reviews were mixed, but Twain was fearless and unguarded in her songwriting and her willingness to experiment sonically. Each track seemed to reveal a snapshot of Twain in various states of grief, rage, self-pity, heartbreak, and hope. It's messy and almost cringingly revealing at times, but it's achingly real

5 Jon Caramanica, "Shania Twain Walked Out on Top. Now She Wants Back In," *New York Times*, September 1, 2017, https://www.nytimes.com/2017/09/01/arts/music/shania-twain-now-interview.html.

and relatable. The circumstances of Twain's divorce were almost cliché, but also, if it could happen to her, it could happen to anybody. *Now* was Twain's catharsis, and in her 2022 documentary, *Not Just a Girl*, she said it was the only album of hers that she still enjoyed listening to. It was hers and hers alone, and that was the empowerment she needed to move forward with her life.

By 2017, Twain's vocal cord problems had worsened, and eventually Twain revealed her voice issues were related to her diagnosis of Lyme disease. In 2018, she underwent a llaryngoplasty, which required her to have stabilizers implanted in her throat. The surgery worked, and through physical therapy, Twain resumed performing and eventually agreed to tell her story through the aforementioned documentary. (Full disclosure, I had a conversation with the director and was asked to participate, but due to the pandemic, I had to decline.) When I finally watched *Not Just a Girl*, I was fascinated. In the last few years, the bio-doc genre has been an incredible space for many famous women to correct the historical record and use their voices to write themselves back into the public record and history. These bio-docs typically humanize their subjects and empower them to tell their own stories and challenge the sexist, misogynist, racist, ageist, and ableist public and critical discourse. From Taylor Swift's *Miss Americana* and Brooke Shields's *Pretty Baby* and Pamela Anderson's *Pamela: A Love Story* to Sheryl Crow's *Sheryl* and Mary J. Blige's *My Life* and Buffy Sainte-Marie's *Carry It On*, there are countless stories of women whose contributions were erased, ignored, and/or invalidated, deemed too much or too little, and trivialized because of their gender.

Not Just a Girl opens with Twain's narration: "I believe that every great leader of their own destiny is fearless. There is no other way to be. Aware but fearless. I am going to make my own decisions in life, and I'm going to make my own money. I'm going to buy my own car and make my own way. I'm not going to depend on anybody else. The minute you depend on somebody else, you lose something. You lose the right to decide for yourself. You just got to go for it. Taking the risks to do things your way can be scary, so you gotta be brave."[6] It's less a speech and more like a series of thoughts she dashed off at various points in her life and then strung together for this moment, but fifteen-year-old me is wishing she'd seen this side of Twain. Present-day me concurs with parts of what she says, but the rest of me aches for her because Twain's wounds, from childhood to adulthood, have never fully healed and it's evident that depending on someone else is a concept that she still can't embrace. I know the abandonment that triggers outsized independence, but thankfully I also know the love and community that made me realize otherwise. Maybe Twain's happiness really is rooted in independence, not interdependence. I genuinely want her to be living her best life, which is something I could not have predicted being emotionally invested in 1995.

The documentary gives Twain the space and credit she deserves for the role she played in her own success. Of course, the kind of unprecedented success she had was a group effort, nobody, least of all Twain, has ever said it wasn't, but she's the only artist to have three albums in a row go diamond (selling over ten million copies). That is wild. Not only, obviously, did she sing, tour, perform, do all the interviews, co-write the songs, and help produce them, but according to Twain and plenty of secondary

6 *Shania Twain: Not Just a Girl*, directed by Joss Crowley, 2022.

sources in the doc, she was chiefly responsible for the aesthetic of Shania Twain: she wanted the bare midriffs, she co-designed her outfits, came up with the concepts and looks for her music videos, and then edited the raw footage! Her agency was in every frame, and it was there in most of the lyrics, too, if you were listening. "She might not wear a banner on her hat that says, 'I'm a feminist,'" Bo Derek says in *Not Just a Girl*. "She just did it."

I would love it if Twain was a self-declared feminist, but Derek is right. She doesn't have to claim the label for her music and her actions to have a progressive, inclusive effect. The doc briefly touches on Twain's large LGBTQ+ following. "Anybody that sees that level of confidence and self-ownership and comes from a place of struggle and oppression is completely turned on by that," journalist Eve Barlow says in *Not Just a Girl*. "Because that is their permission to flaunt it in exactly the same way as Shania does." And Twain doesn't shy away from collaborating with younger, queer artists, either. She joined forces with the frequently masked, openly gay Canadian alt-country artist Orville Peck in 2020 for the song "Legends Never Die," which Peck wrote for her as a duet. "She reached through the stereo and made me feel, I guess, safe when I was a young kid," Peck tells the documentarians.

Twain has especially come into her own since 2022. She hints at her evolution in *Not Just a Girl*. "I'm swinging back into this space of — I don't even want to say female empowerment, but self-empowerment," Twain says as the documentary comes to a close. "I'm just feeling good in my own skin and less apologetic than ever." In 2023, Twain released her newest album, *Queen of Me*, a record that is more raucous and confident than *Now* and more playful, too. There are a few country-pop crossover songs, including the campily perfect opener, "Giddy Up!," while the rest of the album is more deliberately pop-forward. She's feeling herself throughout, and there's a high sass factor befitting the album's title, all of which seems to be influencing her aesthetics on red carpets, at awards shows, and on tour. Some critics have balked at Twain's "new" penchant for wild wigs and campy outfits that seem more like cosplay than couture, but she has always played with her presentation. High camp is her visual love language, and she has a knack for transforming the ridiculous into the iconic, such as her "That Don't Impress Me Much" music video look: full leopard print head to toe, with just a half mile of abs to complement the hooded cape, bra, skin-tight pants, and boots. How is that not an indicator that maybe thirty years later she'd up the ante?

These are just three of the vivid, vibrant looks that trained all eyes on Twain yet again: a platinum blond, middle-parted wig hanging straight and wispy to her chest and a shiny, silk rust-orange outfit; waist-length, banged, neon-red hair and a shiny bell-bottom suit in a large polka dot cow print with a domed, two-foot-high, massively brimmed matching hat; and bubble-gum pink, banged, and feathery shoulder-length layered hair under another leopard print hood, but instead of a cape flowing down her back, the two sides of leopard print fabric folded across her shoulders like a large bow and spilled down the backs of her arms. This is in combination with the full mesh top that extended over her arms and hands but strategically under the leopard print strapless bra, and the long black velvet skirt that pooled over her feet with a waistline v-cut to frame her belly button and point down like an arrow to her razzle-dazzle. Twain was back in all her glory, damn the numerous headlines that touted her as "unrecognizable" or "nearly unrecognizable." (A quick Google of "Shania Twain unrecognizable" returned more than 26,000 results in .41 seconds on Thursday, August 3, 2023, at 8:30 p.m. PT.)

Twain, it seems, does not give a shit, which is perfect. This state of mind has been decades in the making. "It's like a renaissance period for me. To be experiencing it as a relevant artist still, that's rewarding," Twain told *People* in 2022. "I feel a renewed confidence. I don't have anything to prove anymore, and I feel freedom in that."[7] When *Queen of Me* was released, she returned to performing, marrying her new looks with some timeless classics; Twain even embraced avant-garde high fashion for a 2023 *In Style* photo spread. After years of being something of a style provocateur, Twain was ready to level up: "I love it. I'm so up for it . . . I'm way more fearless than I would've been. Years ago, I would've been more conscientious about, 'Is this too over-the-top?' I'm more adventurous now and I'm just excited about what is new and what I can experiment with. I just love fashion for that. Just when you think there's nothing left to be created, somebody creates something new. I'm so inspired by that. When you can transform a living person just by putting something on, it's spectacular."[8]

In press interviews supporting *Queen of Me*, Twain opened up repeatedly about her image and her body. She had controlled her image as Shania Twain but had never quite felt comfortable

7 Jeff Nelson, "Shania Twain on Reclaiming Her Throne: 'I Don't Have Anything to Prove Anymore,'" *People*, December 20, 2022, https://people.com/country/shania-twain-reclaiming-throne-after-heartbreak-health-setbacks/.

8 Christopher Luu, "Shania Twain Says Her Songs Belong to Everybody," *In Style*, January 19, 2023, https://www.instyle.com/shania-twain-cover-interview-7096246.

in her own private skin, not as Shania. "I feel strongly about wearing my truth on my sleeve, with joy," Twain told *Toronto Life* in 2023. "Otherwise, you lose that moment. I spent so many years hiding my body instead of celebrating it, and what a waste that was. I should have been enjoying it! Time is the only thing that we have to lose — I'm only this age right now."[9] As Twain told *In Style*, she no longer worries the way she did when she was younger. "I'm a professional. I want things to be great. I want to be as perfect as I can be as a professional, but I'm not a perfect person. I sound different. I look different and I'm OK with that. I'm fearless in that way and that motivates me."[10]

Twain is also carrying this new energy into her long-awaited return to Las Vegas. The Come on Over residency — Twain's third Vegas residency — kicks off May 2024 and will highlight Twain's "obsession" with fashion. "I don't know where this energy is coming from right now," Twain told *People*. "I mean, maybe it's gratitude. I think it's a combination of gratitude and confidence . . . I've got just more self-confidence. Self-doubt, I just don't have time for that. I would rather be wrong and make a mistake but still be moving forward than to be stuck or fenced in by fear or self-doubt."[11]

Shania Twain is, at long last, queen of herself.

---

9 Stephanie Verge, "The Making of a Superstar," *Toronto Life*, June 19, 2023, https://torontolife.com/deep-dives/shania-twain-on-her-years-dreaming-big-in-toronto/.

10 Luu, "Shania Twain Says."

11 Mark Gray, "Shania Twain Launching 'Come on Over' Vegas Residency Show, Plans to Showcase Her 'Obsession' with Fashion (Exclusive)," *People*, August 15, 2023, https://people.com/shania-twain-come-on-over-vegas-residency-show-exclusive-7643419.

ALANIS MORISSETTE, *JAGGED LITTLE PILL*, AND 1995

What It Feels Like for a Girl

Alanis Morissette sort of saved my life.

She didn't catch me after a six-storey drop or pull me back from stepping out in front of a train. But the release of her record *Jagged Little Pill* in 1995 afforded me a permission I didn't even know I needed. It gave me a voice, and as a teenaged girl, it wasn't just exciting, it was liberating.

"Oh, man," Morissette once told the *New York Times*. "I wish I had me to listen to when I was fourteen."[1]

I totally get that. After all, I felt like she'd crawled out from inside my sixteen-year-old head, that she was the external manifestation of my alter ego. She asked the same questions I'd been asking. She felt things I was feeling: silenced, dismissed, frustrated, fucked over, betrayed, heartbroken, spurned, sad, foolish, flawed, hopeful. I felt like I wasn't alone. When we find art and music and culture that reflects our inner lives, that's the moment

1 Jon Pareles, "At Lunch With: Alanis Morissette; Better to Sing the Teen-Age Life Than Live It," *New York Times*, February 28, 1996, https://www.nytimes.com/1996/02/28/garden/at-lunch-with-alanis-morissette-better-to-sing-the-teen-age-life-than-live-it.html.

we flip from enthusiasts to true fans — when we find ourselves in and changed by art, not simply appreciative of its existence.

Our society makes it commonplace to dismiss and silence teenaged girls, but in 1995, there was no refuge from Morissette's reach, and it was empowering. *Jagged Little Pill* sounded like freedom and catharsis; I loved it. It wasn't pretty, not always, nor was it soft all the time. It was ugly, sexy, vulnerable, and honest. The album is hugely produced, overproduced even, but it felt unadorned compared to the polish of some of her contemporaries. The theatrics seeped out of every enunciation, like she was channelling a feral beast, a wildling — how girls and women sometimes sounded on the inside, where no one could hear us. It was the sound of both total abandon and calculated emotional manipulation, another seeming contrast that is really an obvious and commonplace duality.

Yet Morissette had to duck a hefty number of accusations about her authenticity, including some from the Canadian media, which, according to Morissette in a 1995 *Rolling Stone* interview, pointed out her pop past and said her "records sucked and that what I'm now doing is contrived."[2] Courtney Love accused Madonna — the head of Maverick Records, Morissette's label — of manufacturing Morissette to strip alternative music of its credibility. *Entertainment Weekly* quoted a Minneapolis DJ who, in introducing an Everclear song, ranted, "This is like the anti-Alanis. This is by a band that wasn't manufactured but

---

2 David Wild, "Alanis Morissette: The Adventures of Miss Thing," *Rolling Stone*, November 2, 1995, https://www.rollingstone.com/music/music-news/alanis-morissette-the-adventures-of-miss-thing-53743/.

actually worked hard, recorded, and toured for years to get some success."[3]

Totally, dude. Sure, Everclear worked super hard.

What this DJ overlooked was that Morissette was already a veteran of both show business and the music business by seventeen, appearing on *You Can't Do That on Television* and releasing two forgettable dance-pop albums — forgettable in that one went platinum but only in Canada — under only her first name. It's a testament to her work ethic that she managed to completely reinvent herself as the best-selling artist in the world by twenty-one. But she was just a girl so she must not have known shit, right? Or she was just an aggro-Barbie industry plant. "Angry chick" became a way to both dismiss and exult Morissette, like when the *New York Daily News* wrote that almost all of *Jagged Little Pill* expressed a "near-volcanic rage" and that "the result, at times, can seem like a desperate cry for attention in a pop world already ratcheted high."[4] To this day, there are tongue-waggers who deem Morissette too aggressive, too vulgar, and too irate; who label her "unladylike" because she dared give voice — loudly — to her vexations.

That was 1995. In 2015, when the first edition of this book was published, some women were compelled to start a campaign banning the word "bossy" because women are still thought to be difficult if they are demanding or dissatisfied or if they communicate their displeasure.

---

3 Chris Willman and John Bream, "The Quiet Riot Grrrl," *Entertainment Weekly*, March 15, 1996, https://research.ebsco.com/c/vggnxk/viewer/html/aqer6ovr6f.

4 "Lust Never Sleeps: Morissette Gives Candid Sex Talk a New Edge," *New York Daily News*, July 24, 1995, https://www.nydailynews.com/1995/07/24/lust-never-sleeps-morissette-gives-candid-sex-talk-a-jagged-new-edge/.

Morissette was the poster child for "bossy" or an "angry chick," a narrative that both garnered her adulation from fans and perpetuated a sexist, misogynistic view with which critics could minimize and devalue *Jagged Little Pill*'s importance. But dismissing Morissette's anger was somewhat de rigueur for those who couldn't or wouldn't acknowledge their own privilege within the established good-ol'-boy gate-kept music industry. In acknowledging only Morissette's anger, they attempted to invalidate it and by extension her, and once they reduced her to that angry chick stereotype, she quickly became a punchline. And once that was accomplished, the hierarchy of who wielded power in the music industry and who didn't was, once again, safely upheld.

Was Morissette angry? Yes, definitely. Anybody would have been, considering what she experienced between the ages of fourteen and eighteen. Years later, she would go on the record, detailing the events she had alluded to throughout *Jagged Little Pill*: when she was fourteen years old, she had a sexual relationship with a twenty-nine-year-old man in the music industry. In 2002, she released a song about the relationship called "Hands Clean" and told *Newsweek*, "I did it for the sake of my being liberated at long last. Whether you call it statutory rape or inappropriate behavior by an adult — it doesn't matter. I didn't do it to have him charged or called out on the carpet. I wanted to tell the truth to myself. I felt at the time I had only two choices — I pick either working with this person or not doing music at all. Hopefully some 16-year-old can think of me for even 10 milliseconds and realize they're not alone or crazy."[5]

5 Lorraine Ali, "Alanis Is Cleaning House," *Newsweek*, March 4, 2002.

The record label also pressured her to lose weight during that time, warning Morissette she couldn't be successful and fat. She subsequently battled both bulimia and anorexia until she sought help from a therapist at age seventeen. It's important to emphasize this: she was seventeen years old and she had to get *herself* into therapy despite the fact that she was surrounded by adults. The majority of the adults in Morissette's teenage life were much more focused on exploitation and getting what they wanted from her — sexually, financially, creatively, egotistically — than supporting her artistic vision or caring for her as a human.

Morissette finally extracted herself from that toxic situation when she was eighteen years old. She sought new collaborators and ultimately aligned herself with a producer who pushed her to explore the pent-up frustration and trauma of her youth. He wanted to hear what she had to say, and Morissette managed to find some semblance of satisfaction and maybe even some healing by ripping the words from the darkest corners of her psyche.

That's one reason this record resonated so deeply for so many people: songs like hers weren't just "fuck you" tunes, they were vindication anthems. They illustrated a potential universe wherein turning one's back on the status quo, particularly a status quo that perpetuated huge imbalances of power, would ultimately result in victory — the sweet relief of triumphing over the bastards that tried to hold you down. And Morissette got her revenge according to a 1995 *Spin* profile that detailed a *Jagged Little Pill* showcase at Toronto's Lee's Palace. "After the show, she tells me that she spotted in the audience some of the same record execs who inspired the song. Her eyes light up.

'When this one guy approached me backstage,' she whispers, 'I looked him in the eye and said, "See you on the way down."'"[6]

Morissette wrote the bulk of *Jagged Little Pill*'s songs before she turned twenty. The record was born out of the scorched earth of a sexed-up pop image, an earlier failed record, and a seemingly endless supply of predatory older men who had attempted to exploit/capitalize on/crush the "it" factor right out of her. But Morissette was smart, clever, and strong, which was something those early career record executives hadn't counted on. Little girls don't grow up to have backbones, foul mouths, and opinions, right? Oh, Mr. Man, you're always such a goddamned fool.

Here are two truths about Alanis Morissette: she was a prolific songwriter from the age of eight, and she wanted fame and stardom, or at least to be the centre of attention.

In 1983, John Alexander, the head of A&R at MCA Records, passed on Morissette's demo tape. He praised her voice but asked, "What am I going to do with a nine-year-old?" In 1986, Morissette was cast on YTV's *You Can't Do That on Television*. She made enough money to record her first song with family friend and mentor Lindsay Morgan, who was also a musician. In 1988, producer Leslie Howe and entertainment manager Stephan Klovan decided to help Morissette get her first record contract. This time, Alexander signed her, and *Alanis*, a record heavy on dance-pop clichés, was released in 1991.

6 James Hannaham, "Alanis in Wonderland," *Spin*, November 1995, https://www.spin.com/featured/alanis-morissette-jagged-little-pill-november-1995-cover-story-alanis-in-wonderland/.

The debut single, "Too Hot," was a huge success as was the video that features her dancing, caressing, and grinding on the dudes in her dance posse. She's wearing a leather jacket, jeans, and a black bra. She's barely sixteen but looks like she's staring down the barrel of thirty. The sexed-up dance-pop muscle is fully flexed on the entire record, right from the first track, "Feel Your Love," and the chorus that promises to give and receive. Subtle, right? *Alanis* was certified platinum, and Morissette was an instant hit. Or, at the very least, people called her the "Debbie Gibson of Canada," though, let's be clear, her videos had much more in common with Paula Abdul than Gibson and, perhaps, laid the foundation for Britney Spears and her exploitation at the opposite end of the decade.

Morissette's dance-pop career was short-lived, however. Her second record, 1992's *Now Is the Time*, went heavier on the ballads and subsequently tanked. "Everyone around me was horrified. But I was happy," she told CNN.[7] At eighteen years old, Morissette was free of her contract and ready to start over. She moved from Ottawa to Toronto and picked up the guitar. For the next year, she collaborated with more than one hundred musicians before heading to L.A., where she met producer Glen Ballard in 1994.

"I thought wow, here's someone I can delve into some subject matters that may offend, or trigger, or bother some other collaborators," Morissette told CNN. "Glen was embracing it; and he was saying, 'Keep on, let's do it.'"[8]

---

7 Kyra Phillips, "People in the News," CNN, January 4, 2003, https://transcripts.cnn.com/show/pitn/date/2003-01-04/segment/00.

8 Phillips, "People in the News."

Ballard encouraged Morissette to be honest above all else, and she responded by digging into the things that had been threatening to derail her: self-esteem issues, body dysmorphia, fucked-up power dynamics with powerful men, statutory rape, bad relationships, anxiety, and an inferiority complex. It would be years before she discussed the details explicitly, but over the space of a few weeks collaborating with Ballard, she lit her dance-pop past on fire and from its ashes wrote one of the most iconic albums of the '90s.

That first line of *Jagged Little Pill* is among the greatest, most telling, perfect first lines of any record in the '90s. It sets the stage for everything that follows: the tension, inclusivity, contemporary self-absorption — it's all encapsulated in the way Morissette spits out those five words, forming an angry, snarky, pointed question that doesn't require an answer. Her tone is frank, mocking, not at all conciliatory but not self-aggrandizing, either. The deliberate way in which she phrases the question sucks the listener inside the song, even if they are a reluctant participant.

From the first track, "All I Really Want," Morissette establishes a specific voice, one that takes pleasure in rejecting "normal" lyrical patterns or vocal maneuvers. She juxtaposes poetic images, two-dollar words, broad concepts (apathy, deliverance, the black hole of solitary depression), and pointed observations that she serves up in a whiplash assortment of vocal tics, tricks, and distortion: strangled cries, growls and grunts, a crescendoing alto, snarled frustration, sexy assertiveness, pained experience, and youthful confidence.

"You Oughta Know" starts quietly; it turns your ears up and beckons your brain closer while the volume slowly climbs, ebbing and flowing between the verses and choruses. A series of great lines acknowledge the betrayal, fury, and self-destruction that accompany a bad breakup but levelled up with an unapologetic frankness to talk about fucking, a public blow job, and other sexual imagery in a mainstream radio hit.

It's easy to think that the flow of the record is a reflection of Morissette's impulsive nature or recklessness, but following up those two tracks with the quiet, killer "Perfect" illustrates the mastery of *JLP*'s sequencing. "Perfect" is a brilliant mirror reflecting the ways in which whole lives and psyches unravel in moments of upheaval, affording us an opportunity to examine all the parts of ourselves that have led us to pivotal moments of personal reckoning. How do we get to places where we let other people make us feel like shit? Why don't we stand up and fight for ourselves? Why is it so much easier to demand great things for our friends and loved ones but not always ourselves? "Perfect" examines those feelings with self-awareness and clarity. It is exploring the pressure of performance, living up to expectations, and the ways in which you can end up totally alienated, alone, and feeling like a complete failure. It starts softly and then explodes; while it may seem over the top, that moment forges the relationship between the listener and the record.

The few seconds of space between "Perfect" and "Hand in My Pocket" don't just give us a chance to catch our breath, they signal a sea change: we're putting the last three songs to bed and moving forward to a place where Morissette is fully self-possessed and confident. That confidence propels the album in an incredible direction with "Right through You," wherein

Morissette calls out a shadowy oppressor, taunting him for his failure and his inability to silence and suppress her. She imagines a future in which she has not just survived but is thriving, gloriously living her best life.

It's wish fulfillment of the highest order, but it is also catharsis and inspiration, themes Morissette continues to explore on "Forgiven" and "You Learn," songs that attempt to contextualize reckonings, both religious and emotional. To dismantle the pieces of our lives that shape us and subsequently fail us, to acknowledge the stuff that fucks us up, the dubious hypocrisy of sexism and patriarchy — that's big, meaty stuff. It's intoxicating because Morissette knows that silence is suffocation. Every lyric about faith, hypocrisy, and absolution in "Forgiven" is like a gnarled branch fighting for the cathartic and redemptive light of "You Learn."

The sweetness of "Head over Feet," the sensitive sprawl of "Mary Jane," and the quirky landscape of "Ironic" were baffling to the easily confused, particularly those who insisted on seeing Morissette in one dimension: a screaming, seething ball of rage. *How can she be so angry but so gentle here?* Well, how can you have both a right hand and a left hand? It's simple, provided you're not someone who hates women. People contain multitudes, and women are people; therefore women contain multitudes. This fact is still often treated as a new concept today, just as it was in 1995. Pop star Olivia Rodrigo has been labelled "angry" ever since her 2021 smash hit "drivers license" reached number one on the Billboard charts and stayed there for eight consecutive weeks. In fact, Google her name plus "angry" and there are more than four million hits returned in .35 seconds. Rodrigo herself has willingly talked about her anger and rage, but it's not the only emotion in her music.

"Not the Doctor" is the best marriage of Morissette's insight, wit, and mastery of one-liners. Every statement is ultra-specific yet universal, a little truth bomb to the ego of every man who's ever demanded that she be anything other than an equal partner. Her refusal to do emotional labour or take responsibility for the man's failure of identity is important. So is her decisive declaration: I can't fix you. She gives many reasons for this, but here are my personal highlights: she doesn't want to be the person's mother because she didn't carry them in her womb for nine months, nor does she want to be someone's other half because she believes in math.

"Wake Up," the second to last song on *Jagged Little Pill*'s tracklist, is the weakest on the album, but even it contains resonant moments, particularly as the song calls out some of the worst aspects of gendered privilege and gender inequality. That it ends on the titular words "wake up" and then immediately dives back into a second version of "You Oughta Know" is a bold move. It reinforces the importance of the track and makes the listener feel like they've come full circle.

But Morissette has one last card to play, and she knows the benefits of silence, the tension that manifests in the absence of words and the anticipation that builds in the delayed gratification of a conclusive end: the "secret song." To this day, a secret song or an unlisted track feels like an especially '90s delight, and I remember being absolutely stunned the first time I heard Morissette's contribution to this small but sometimes mighty canon.

After the second "You Oughta Know" finishes, the track doesn't end. It keeps going and the silence almost vibrates in anticipation. And then suddenly Morissette's voice appears like a shaft of sunshine pouring through the crack of an open door. Her quietly broken a cappella is flooring after all of *Jagged Little Pill*'s vocal tricks and contortions. I've always thought of "Your House" as the story of a woman visiting her lover's home while he is out (she walks through the door, she doesn't break in). Their relationship is shaky, perhaps the power dynamic is unequal, and she gets her heart broken as swift punishment for invading his privacy. It's devastating. Morissette's vocal delivery is what wrenched me in half upon discovering the secret track. It's a worthy, amazing surprise at the end of an already pivotal record.

Prior to the release of *Jagged Little Pill*, Morissette had been grossly underestimated. She'd been summarily dismissed. Powerful men in music had attempted to make her into what they wanted and to profit off their creation. Morissette had other plans, and a hell of a lot to say about a lot of subjects. It wasn't just girl power that Morissette manifested, though that was inspiring in and of itself; rather she became a voice for the disenfranchised, someone who fired back at the men who wanted to keep her down. She crushed them by standing up for herself, by refusing to apologize for all the things that supposedly make women weak.

The irony, of course, is somewhat delicious since Morissette turned every terrible experience of her four-year-long pop music shit show into the epic, eccentric, electric *Jagged Little Pill*, which really was its own revolution. It wasn't just about anger, but anger was part of its emotional spectrum and Morissette's own experiences. So many people are denied their anger or have their anger invalidated by stereotyping, cultural clichés, racism, sexism, ageism, or classism. As a teenaged girl, I was particularly aware of this silencing and how it led to my self-censorship: it's not ladylike to get angry; getting angry makes too many other people feel bad; getting angry is a waste of time; don't get angry, get even; anger just makes you look stupid.

But listening to *Jagged Little Pill*, it felt good to indulge in a bit of anger after years of suppressing any feelings of outrage in favour of being a "good" girl. Morissette made me feel comfortable expressing my anger. But to only use "angry" to describe her or *Jagged Little Pill* is missing the point. Her character is much more complex. Sure, "angry" is part of it, but that one note couldn't sustain an entire song, never mind a record that inspired multiple generations and still resonates three decades later. Song by song, line by line, the wry, vulnerable, heartbroken, and defiant moments outnumber the snarled, hateful "fuck yous" two to one. On *JLP*, Morissette dares us to feel our feelings and makes it clear that we're entitled to much more than a narrow, limited experience determined by our age or gender.

The 1995 *Spin* cover story revealed that when it came to the ways women are pigeon-holed, precious little had changed since first- and second-wave feminism:

> Morissette mines the nitty-gritty too often relegated to mere subtext in pop music. Grrrls can't be girls because the media defines them through

> their anger, and that just makes them angrier. The way in which Morissette carves out space for a broad emotional range is more typical of men: she simply assumes it. "Being able to express both your masculine and feminine sides is a great advantage," asserts the former tomboy. Morissette's gentler (but not necessarily "feminine") side, as heard on "Hand in My Pocket" and the sympathetic "Mary Jane," nestled alongside rants like "You Oughta Know," effects a sea change in pop music by affirming that "angry" and "woman" don't have to add up to "angry woman."[9]

There's a lot in here that reinforces the very narratives and tropes the writer seems to want to dismantle. "Grrrls can't be girls" — don't. This whole sentence is both a self-fulfilling prophecy and the written equivalent of a snake eating its own tail. "Broad emotional range is more typical of men: she simply assumes it" — same. A broad emotional range is not more typical of men, and plenty of women have assumed it without the same level of success as Morissette. The entire Riot Grrrl movement had been going strong for years at this point. "The former tomboy" — seriously, this is too much. "Affirming that 'angry' and 'woman' don't have to add up to 'angry woman'" — I get what the writer's doing. I do. But it's not only okay to be angry and a woman, it's actually totally fucking fine to be an angry woman. Because that's not the sum total of a person; that's just a fraction of the aspect ratio, one swatch in the Pantone Color Systems.

9 Hannaham, "Alanis in Wonderland."

Among my earliest fictional role models were Miss Piggy and Murphy Brown. Miss Piggy is a diva whose outsized fabulousness masks some genuine insecurity, and Murphy Brown is a fiercely intelligent career woman, and though she doesn't suffer fools gladly, she's occasionally brought down by her own hubris. Despite both being fictional (and one a Muppet), they've been categorized as "angry women" at one point or another. Two of my favourite songwriters in my early teens, Liz Phair and Courtney Love, were also considered "angry women." In fact, I could fill this entire book only with names of women who have inspired me in some way, and ninety-five percent of them have been tagged as "angry women" at varying points in their careers. I've been called an "angry woman" more times than I can count, and I can also feel it on the tips of some tongues when I'm in professional meetings with certain people. Assertive = difficult = "angry woman."

This description crosses all mediums and platforms and penetrates every aspect of a woman's identity in tangible and intangible ways. "Angry woman" aims to diminish and silence voices that threaten the status quo. "Angry woman" falsely disqualifies femininity. "Angry woman" perpetuates stereotypes of man-hating, humourless, nagging, tiring hags. "Angry woman" presumes jokes are crafted from a level playing field. "Angry woman" subsumes angry women every time; it is the dog whistle of misogynists and sexists who justify ignoring our voices in defence of themselves or their allies.

I owe it to myself to embrace the angry woman moments of my emotional spectrum. The next time I'm worried about being "too annoying" or "not fun" or "kind of a bitch," I'll ask myself, *If I wasn't a woman, would stating my need or opinion even be an issue?* It's time to call bullshit and stop accepting sexist microaggressions as "it is what it is" or whatever other meaningless corporate platitude we're asked to swallow as a substitute for meaningful change. I am done with apologizing for being a real person with reasonable needs.

***

Morissette also had to battle accusations that she was inauthentic, just a calculated invention of the label and Glen Ballard to capitalize on the rise of women singer-songwriters. Despite, or because of, *Jagged Little Pill*'s blockbuster status, there was a lot of talk attempting to recontextualize and minimize Morissette's success. *Jagged Little Pill* was all hype, no substance; Morissette was a fraud; the whole record was sentimental revenge histrionics, cheese of the highest order, from a crazy chick, etc.

As Morissette's fame grew, so did the target on her back. Consider the gleeful delight with which people focused mercilessly on "Ironic," writing extensively about how Morissette obviously didn't even know the meaning of the word. *Entertainment Weekly*'s Casey Davidson describes the situation as a "defining moment":

> And the latest hot topic of radio talk around the country is — semantics? Pop's reigning angry woman, Alanis Morissette, is causing an all-out airwave debate over a simple adjective with her top 10 single "Ironic." The singer seems to define the word improperly . . . DJs and other linguists are quick to point out that her musings should be filed under annoying or coincidental, not ironic. "I'd say Joan Osborne's 'One of Us' has a hell of

> a lot of irony," says Susan Willis, associate professor of English at Duke University. "But what Alanis is singing about is a bunch of bummers." On the other hand, a song called "Bummer" just wouldn't have quite the same ring.[10]

I'm a stickler for definitions, too, but the number of people who jumped down Morissette's throat for "Ironic" far outweighed the number of people who actually care about linguistics. It felt like a swell of people simply hated her and her music and wanted to see a young woman knocked down off her pedestal, especially a young woman who seemed to have achieved success by being unashamed of her feelings and putting the men who'd hurt her on blast. Morissette became famous, yes, and one cynical way to look at it could be to say that she benefitted from exploiting her own suffering. But that would be overlooking the real sacrifice in her musical catharsis and the substantial rewards that she earned.

Morissette had almost no childhood. "I started writing songs when I was nine and started a record company when I was ten," she told *Forbes* in 2019. "That's when I started meeting with lawyers and producers and started the active part of my professional life in earnest. I started learning what conference calls were, about legal conversations and what publishing meant. As you know, these were the first few steps toward a well-honed work addiction. I started feeling like my sense of self was best defined through my work. There are pros and cons to that. The

10 Casey Davidson, "Hot Flashes," *Entertainment Weekly*, April 19, 1996, https://ew.com/article/1996/04/19/flashes-74/.

self-expression aspect is a boon and exciting, but the overwork aspect is a little hard on the nervous system and turns into a full-blown addiction."[11]

When *Jagged Little Pill* turned Morissette into an overnight sensation in America, her work addiction went into overdrive. "There was a period of time during the *Jagged Little Pill* era where I don't think I laughed for about two years," Morissette recalled in a 2012 interview with *The Guardian*. "It was a survival mode, you know. It was an intense, constant, chronic over-stimulation and invasion of energetic and physical literal space."[12]

Morissette poured the gasoline and her listeners lit the match because they identified with her struggles and triumphs — the shit and the sorrow and the fury and the fun and the love. She spoke about the complexities of women, specifically young women, in ways that others didn't. She was a role model in a much more literal sense than someone like Céline Dion. Dion was something to aspire to, a perfection that was just out of reach, while Morissette was a peer, someone who had made it out alive and didn't mind taking a wrecking ball to the worst and best of being a girl.

***

---

11 Bryan Robinson, "'I Used To Think I Was Invincible': Alanis Morissette Talks Burnout Prevention and Her Journey to Work-Life Balance," *Forbes*, November 1, 2019, https://www.forbes.com/sites/bryanrobinson/2019/11/01/singersongwriter-alanis-morissettes-multi-tentacled-wellness-gifts-for-the-season.

12 Michael Cragg, "I Still Have PTSD from the Jagged Little Pill Era. It Was a Profound Violation," *Guardian*, August 16, 2012, https://www.theguardian.com/music/2012/aug/16/alanis-morissette-profound-violation.

In December 2019, I saw *Jagged Little Pill* on Broadway in previews, just a day or two before opening night, and it was fucking incredible. Alanis Morissette didn't need to prove the timelessness of her 1995 chart-topping breakthrough, but by reinventing it for Broadway, alongside original *Jagged Little Pill* co-conspirator Glen Ballard and writer Diablo Cody (*Juno*), she did. I love theatre, especially musical theatre, and to see *JLP*'s evolution on the stage — and Broadway at that! — felt like a fever dream of my own design. I didn't even know I'd wished for it until it came true.

That night I wrote about the experience for CBC Music, where I'm an associate producer, and why seeing *JLP* evolve and grow up with me in this way was so meaningful:

> *Jagged Little Pill*'s journey to Broadway probably seems strange to those immune — prescriptively, performatively or genuinely — to its charms. But those of us who have loved it have secretly hoped a day like this would come. The record that helped us love ourselves, forgive ourselves, and see ourselves now has its own second life thanks to *Jagged Little Pill: The Musical*, and a third life, too, with the recently announced 25th anniversary tour next year.
>
> The musical's expansive reimagining of the album's songs is like growing up with a group of friends, all of us stepping into our future selves together. Reaching backwards and forwards through time, growing into deeper understandings together. In revealing new facets of the album's

> depths, the musical also reveals new facets of my love for all of these songs. *Jagged Little Pill* forever.[13]

Morissette insisted that *JLP* the musical tackle big issues with candour: rape and consent, drug, sex, and work addiction disorders, trans-racial adoption and anti-Blackness, body image issues, the opioid crisis, gender identity, sexuality, and self-harm. The *New York Times* called it "the most woke musical since *Hair*."[14] Morissette was asked to remove different topics from the musical, including the rape. "I said, 'Not a f---king chance! We have to put this in or I'm not interested,'" she told the *Sydney Morning Herald*. "I don't think I've actually met a woman who hasn't been subject to some version of it. Even the request for it not to be in the musical is in and of itself a form of erasure."[15]

A few months after *JLP* opened onstage, Covid hit and lockdown began, but Morissette kept busy. Her planned twenty-fifth anniversary *JLP* tour was postponed, but she went ahead with the release of her new album, *Such Pretty Forks in the Road*, on July 31, 2020. It was her first new record in eight years, and it's as provocatively confessional as anything on *JLP*, the anger and vulnerability and joy still present if more contained. In part, it's

---

13 Andrea Warner, "*Jagged Little Pill*: A Love Letter to the Album and the Musical," CBC Music, December 5, 2019, https://www.cbc.ca/music/jagged-little-pill-a-love-letter-to-the-album-and-the-musical-1.5385321.

14 Joshua Barone, "Has Alanis Morissette Made the Most Woke Musical Since 'Hair'?" *New York Times*, May 16, 2018, https://www.nytimes.com/2018/05/16/theater/alanis-morissette-jagged-little-pill-musical.html.

15 Tessa Souter, "'We're going for our own jugulars': Alanis Morissette on Her Confronting Musical," *Sydney Morning Herald*, November 26, 2021, https://www.smh.com.au/culture/music/we-re-going-for-our-own-jugulars-alanis-morissette-on-her-confronting-musical-20211121-p59ap5.html.

the heavy presence of piano on most of the tracks; even when the guitars kick in and the drums kick out, the piano anchors every arrangement. Morissette's vocals still stray, occasionally, into barbed outrage and eviscerating howls, but she's also full of gratitude, warmth, and playfulness.

Most of Morissette's albums feel like acts of survival, and she has been candid with the press throughout her career about the work she does to keep her mental and physical health in check and how songwriting factors into everything. "I used to think that I could write songs and never have to deal with human beings," Morissette told Liz Phair in a 2020 interview for the *L.A. Times*. "I'd be like, 'I'm really angry at that person, so I'm going to go over here in a room and write about it and then never talk to them. It's perfect.' . . . People are like, 'Oh, it must be so healing to write these songs.' It's clarifying, it's empowering, but it doesn't necessarily heal the relationship itself. I'm Canadian, so I'm basically passive-aggressive. I'm kind, friendly, and then I snap. I'm just a cranky little bitch. There's just no way around it."

Morissette and Phair were both labelled "angry young women" in the press — Morissette's 1995 *Rolling Stone* cover screamed "Angry White Female," a weak nod to the term "single white female" — and both women still see the value in anger and making space for it. "Anger gets such a bad rap, and it can be such a beautiful force," Morissette said. "I mean, it helps us say no. It helps us be activists. It helps us stand up for ourselves, for others. Anger's so amazing. It's just that people equate it with something destructive."[16]

---

16 Liz Phair, "Alanis Morissette and Liz Phair Talk Songwriting during an Apocalypse and Rock-Star Self-Care," *L.A. Times*, July 29, 2020, https://www.latimes.com/entertainment-arts/music/story/2020-07-29/alanis-morissette-liz-phair-jagged-little-pill.

Denying women their right to anger is old-school patriarchy at work. It's also sexist and a form of gendered violence. As *The Guardian* pointed out in a 2020 interview with Morissette, she has been singing about acts of male violence and abuse for more than twenty-five years.

> "That's the most depressing thing in the entire world," she admits, laughing. "The themes of pain and division, trust, exploitation, misogyny, lack of integrity, sociopathic personality disorder and narcissism. These are themes I cut my teeth on as a child." To this day, she says, she is still healing from the theft, and from past sexual trauma that she doesn't detail. She feels she could still fall victim to abuse; it is a pattern she wants to break. She is disarmingly fluent in psychology, including the work of Carl Jung and more contemporary academics. "If I didn't have a whole team of therapists throughout my life, I don't think I'd still be here."[17]

In 2022, Morissette alleged another betrayal, but this time it was levelled at the documentary team behind *Jagged*, directed by Alison Klayman. The project began filming with Morissette's full cooperation, but after seeing the first cut, she disavowed it, loudly and publicly. Stating that she had been interviewed when she was especially vulnerable and coping with postpartum depression, Morissette said, "I was lulled into a false sense of

---

17 Eve Barlow, "Alanis Morissette: 'Without Therapy, I Don't Think I'd Still Be Here,'" *Guardian*, July 24, 2020, https://www.theguardian.com/music/2020/jul/24/alanis-morissette-without-therapy-i-dont-think-id-still-be-here.

security and their salacious agenda became apparent immediately upon my seeing the first cut of the film. This is when I knew our visions were in fact painfully diverged. This was not the story I agreed to tell."[18]

I held off on watching *Jagged* until writing this expansion of *We Oughta Know*, because I do think consent-based storytelling is important, and if Morissette feels harmed and manipulated by *Jagged*, I didn't need to be complicit in that. But as a journalist, I also believe that subjects don't get to call all the shots as to how the story is ultimately told. Journalists and documentarians aren't publicists. Consent-based journalism works when the interviewer is completely transparent and creates an environment of trust that's not about exploitation or extraction. There has to be some accountability if journalists and documentarians are causing harm and pushing a specific agenda.

Now that I've seen *Jagged*, I have some ideas around what caused Morissette to denounce it. She is careful to never name names when she discusses her experiences with sexual assault and statutory rape as a young artist just starting out, but the documentary makes some edits and inserts images that seem to finger men she was working with most directly at the time. As a survivor, it's Morissette's decision whether to name her assailants. Nobody else's. It's impossible to know what was in the cut that Morissette saw, but in her statement rebuking *Jagged*, she concluded that the film "includes implications and facts that are simply not true. While there is beauty and some elements of

18 Savannah Walsh, "Alanis Morissette Slams HBO's Doc about Her: 'This Was Not the Story I Agreed to Tell,'" *Vanity Fair*, September 14, 2021, https://www.vanityfair.com/hollywood/2021/09/alanis-morissette-slams-hbo-doc-about-her-this-was-not-the-story-i-agreed-to-tell.

accuracy in this/my story to be sure — I ultimately won't be supporting someone else's reductive take on a story much too nuanced for them to ever grasp or tell."[19]

There are good interviews with Morissette throughout the film, and it's a fascinating snapshot of her heady ascent to superstardom circa *JLP*; it also reflects on the album's legacy and effect on the singer since then. But *Jagged* also touches on things it seems to have little capacity to deal with, such as the admission by Morissette's former bandmate, the late Taylor Hawkins, that he and the other guys in the band were trying to sleep with as many young fans as possible, often luring the girls backstage under the guise that they might get to meet Morissette. According to Hawkins, when she found out about this on tour, Morissette was furious. She's still angry to this day, and her frustration is palpable through the camera. *JLP* is informed, at least in part, by the predatory behaviour of men in the music industry. Her band perpetuating these behaviours by using her name was incongruous and awful, its own gross situational irony. But when Morissette acknowledges how angry she was, she also admits that she didn't ultimately fire or discipline her band in any meaningful way. The weight of that complicity doesn't just seem to sit heavily on her, but it also sits heavily with us, the audience.

In 2022, Morissette released *The Storm before the Calm*, an album she's been leaning into for decades. It's an ambient meditation album that was also released via the Calm app, which

19 Matthew Strauss, "Alanis Morissette Says New Documentary *Jagged* 'Includes Implications and Facts That Are Simply Not True,'" *Pitchfork*, September 14, 2021, https://pitchfork.com/news/alanis-morissette-reportedly-unhappy-with-new-documentary-jagged-wont-attend-premiere/.

feels like a wild bit of marketing but these are the times we live in. Morissette credits making the album with keeping her "super connected and accountable during Covid" when she felt like she was "going to disappear and float away."[20] As Covid became an ongoing concern and endemic, no longer a pandemic, celebrities and entertainers re-emerged and resumed public life, including Morissette. The 2023 CMT Music Awards made the baffling but brilliant decision to feature Morissette and four contemporary women country artists — Lainey Wilson, Ingrid Andress, Madeline Edwards, and Morgan Wade — performing "You Oughta Know." Understanding how systemic sexism has been such a massive gatekeeper in country music — in spite of the unrivaled success of Twain or Taylor Swift — it is an act of joyful catharsis to see the artists on stage singing their hearts out and other women country artists on their feet in the audience, singing along, fists pumping in the air, while probably at least a few white male executives looked on in discomfort.

Morissette's ongoing participation in the '90s revival and women's empowerment continued a month later when she released a cover of "No Return," the theme song for the award-winning TV series *Yellowjackets*, which is set in two timelines: 1996 and 2021. The show centers on the same characters in their two different time periods: as a high school girls' soccer team whose plane crashes in the remote Canadian wilderness and then twenty-five years later as the adult survivors attempt to cope with the trauma from nineteen months stranded

20 Fraser Lewry, "Alanis Morissette Is Releasing a Meditation Album and It All Sounds *Very* Relaxing," *Louder*, May 19, 2022, https://www.loudersound.com/news/alanis-morissette-is-releasing-a-meditation-album-and-it-sounds-very-relaxing.

in the woods. In a statement, Morissette called the original theme song

> perfect . . . It was a little daunting to be asked to reinterpret it but I see parallels between *Yellowjackets* and my perspective while songwriting: the sheer intensity, that going for the jugular with no fear around going for the profane. I've strived my entire career to support the empowerment of women and sensitives, and see the world through the female lens, and what's so wonderful about this show is that each character is allowed to be dynamic and complex as opposed to oversimplified, reduced versions of women. I feel honoured to be a part of the legacy of *Yellowjackets*.[21]

I believe she already was. *Jagged Little Pill* is in *Yellowjackets'* DNA, just as it's foundational to so much of the feminist music and pop culture canon that followed the album's 1995 release. Morissette and *JLP* are always somewhere in the subtext of my own work, and countless musicians, writers, and artists have namechecked her as an influence over the years. "Alanis proved to the music world that all of us were viable," Garbage lead singer Shirley Manson says in *Jagged*. "Only in hindsight am I aware of what Alanis did for every woman that's come up behind her. When you're battling down thirty million doors, that's helping everyone. That's helping every woman have just that little more

21 Alex Young, "Alanis Morissette Shares Her Version of Yellowjackets Theme Song," *Consequence*, April 14, 2023, https://consequence.net/2023/04/alanis-morissette-yellowjackets-theme-song/.

chance of being successful." Another *Jagged* interview subject, KROQ radio music director Lisa Worden, credits Morissette's *JLP* success with sparking another massive moment in '90s pop culture: "Lilith Fair became a thing, and I think Alanis played a huge part in opening that door."

Same, Lisa Worden. Hard same.

THE MYTH AND MAGIC OF SARAH MCLACHLAN

Saint, Sinner, Feminist, Friend, and Funeral Staple

It's impossible to predict the places grief will take you. When considering the five-year window of importance for this book (1993 to 1997), I did not immediately recall the crucial role Sarah McLachlan and her music played in my life during that time. I knew she was important to me and that her music had been a critical part of my youth and in shaping my feminism. I knew it had guided me through heartbreaks and bolstered new friendships while helping me navigate the messy business of ending others. Her music has been part of my life for over thirty years.

In revisiting McLachlan's catalogue for this book, however, I realized I'd forgotten about her 1996 compilation, *Rarities, B-Sides & Other Stuff*. It surprised me since I remember it taking up permanent space in my CD player back then. I pressed play and by the third song, I was back, all the way back, sitting inside a raw, impossible grief. I was crying in a coffee shop, my head down, hiding my face behind a curtain of my own hair while I forced myself to keep writing what I was feeling.

I wasn't just writing a book about coming of age in the grand shadow of four powerful women who would change

Canadian music — and me — forever. I was also writing a book that would take me back to the year my father died.

Sarah McLachlan's music wasn't always a pitch-perfect soundtrack to grief. The McLachlan I fell in love with began as an artist of edgy complexity — tormented, sexy, and adept at wry misery. McLachlan was the hippie, the feminist, the role model, and the wild child all rolled into one. I wasn't aware then what exactly I was responding to, but there was definitely a vicarious thrill about the ways she explored adult themes that resonated deeply with precocious teens like me. Sexual agency and self-esteem, religious exploration, questioning everything, challenging the status quo — every song was a tether from me to her, a place to ground myself against the likes of Céline Dion and Shania Twain.

McLachlan's first record came out in 1988, but it wasn't until she released her third album in 1993 that she became a truly "big deal." *Fumbling Towards Ecstasy* made her a star, and it established her home base, Nettwerk Records, as a significant player among the independent labels. I was fourteen and obsessed. Her lyrics fuelled the love of poetic music I had developed thanks to Leonard Cohen and Joni Mitchell. She tangles words in specific, messy ways, crafting imagery that swallows the listener whole, changing the shape and meaning of a phrase with a twisted, strangled cry or a delicate piano line or a charged growl. *Fumbling Towards Ecstasy* is chaotic, flawed, life-changing perfection, a wonderful, contrasting scruff to the otherwise polished, slick veneer of 1997's *Surfacing* and every record since. To my ears, there's a distinct "Before *Surfacing*" and "After *Surfacing*" sound to a McLachlan record.

As the album that made her hugely famous, *Surfacing* represents a distinct turning point for McLachlan. It's an album full of beauty, but it's also overproduced, particularly when compared to the (excellent) rough edges of *Fumbling Towards Ecstasy*. *Surfacing* was the pivot point where McLachlan's music began to be labelled as "commercial," where she left her indie roots behind and was embraced by the mainstream.

There were upsides to this, of course. McLachlan used her star power to start Lilith Fair, an all-women music festival that enjoyed three years of vibrant success and helped to mainstream the post-post-modern feminist discourse that had begun during the earlier part of the decade with the more overtly political Riot Grrrl movement. McLachlan came up with the idea when she wanted to tour with Paula Cole, but promoters rejected two women on a bill, so McLachlan said "fuck it" and made her own space. In fact, the idea quickly grew so popular that it evolved into a multi-city summer music festival that was one of the top-grossing music festivals throughout its three-year run and proof that outdated ideas upheld by the music industry were rooted in willful sexism and misogyny, not good financial or business sense.

Lilith Fair was a commercial and artistic success, and it was also a win for women and "women in music." Well, it was more of a win for white straight cis women, but there were smaller wins for the queer and racialized women artists as well. Yet despite the '90s being a relatively phenomenal decade for musicians who were women — and the success of Dion, Twain, Morissette, and McLachlan — a general sexism and misogyny persisted (and let's face it, still persists) in mainstream music.

"At radio, three years ago, when Tori Amos' record and mine came out around the same time, it was like, 'We added Tori this week, so we can't add you,' or vice versa," McLachlan told *Entertainment Weekly* in 1997. "It pitted us against each other; it was ridiculous. I think they've come round to realizing they can't ignore it. There's a lot of great music out there, and it's selling, so they better get with the program. People aren't gonna be terrified by hearing two women back-to-back and change the station."[1]

That hasn't changed much in top 40 and country formats. Anecdotally, in the summer of 2014, I heard a man come up to a stage at a huge outdoor street festival, take one look at a band, and say, "Oh, it's a chick band," and walk away before he even heard them play a note. I have heard so many men say variations of that to me or near me countless times over the years. It's an attitude widely accepted by a variety of men, and some women, who also happen to be the key decision-makers in the music industry. It's an attitude we see in film, books, gaming, and media, too. Women's voices are simply not given the same space as men's, and if they are, it's in specialized, myopic worlds: chick-lit, rom-coms, pop music. It's all bullshit, of course, but it persists because it feeds into and supports the status quo: the idea that what men like is universal, but what women like is niche.

In 1997, the idea of an all-women festival was met with skepticism, derision, and plenty of scorn. McLachlan recounted some of it in *Vanity Fair*'s 2019 Lilith Fair oral history: "We did press conferences, and there were always male DJs asking questions like, 'Why do you hate men? What're you doing backstage, sharing makeup tips?' Fuck off! Maybe we are! What's

---

1 David Browne, "Lilith Fair," *Entertainment Weekly*, May 9, 1997.

wrong with that? It irritated the shit out of me."[2] There were homophobic slurs and assumptions tossed at random, as well as church groups who protested Lilith as the festival's namesake due to religious debates about Lilith's very existence (according to medieval Jewish legend, Lilith was Adam's first wife). Some men and women boycotted the festival because it was "reverse sexism" to make the bill exclusively women, women-identified artists, and women-fronted bands.

But for those of us who attended, Lilith Fair was a transformative experience. So much of what happened between 1993 and 1997 led to Lilith Fair. There was a glorious momentum happening for artists who were also women: the records were selling, the consumer culture had diversified, people were listening to the music women made, and when women were told no, that's not the way it's done, they said "fuck that" and did it themselves.

Sexism and misogyny were still principal foundations of the music industry; that's why McLachlan (and countless others before her) faced programmers who refused to book tours with women-fronted acts — "no all chick bills" — and ridiculous radio rules like music programmers never playing two women in a row. Those rules — largely unspoken but still followed — were pervasive in the industry and in some cases persist to this day. In 2015, a male country music radio consultant said that if people wanted to raise ratings in country radio, they needed to stop playing women. "Females," he said, "they're just not the lettuce in our salad. The lettuce is Luke Bryan and Blake Shelton,

2 Jessica Hopper, with Sasha Geffen and Jenn Pelly, "Building a Mystery: An Oral History of Lilith Fair," *Vanity Fair*, September 30, 2019, https://www.vanityfair.com/style/2019/09/an-oral-history-of-lilith-fair.

Keith Urban and artists like that. The tomatoes of our salad are the females."[3] The outrage was spectacular, and country radio has continued to come under fire for its sexist and outdated programming, though change has been willfully, deliberately slow.

But even in 1997, there was an obvious appetite for more women artists, which was further evident in Lilith Fair attendance and record sales: people wanted music made by women, and women wanted there to be space for women's voices and stories. In 1997, *Rolling Stone*'s Gerri Hirshey wrote: "Lilith's success and its fragmented fair-goers proved two things about female artists today. First, there is a lively market for competent, thoughtful music performed in a kinder, gentler venue . . . Second, and more important, there is no such thing as monolithic Women's Music. There never was nor will there ever be. In fact, if the current high-water mark of women in rock has afforded anything to future generations of artists, it's the chance to venture even further afield. Theirs will be a wider range of choices, from available venues to basic tools."[4]

It's at least partly thanks to McLachlan, who also helped usher in a new era of singer-songwriters with attitude — folk musicians who stretched into electronic, avant-pop, chamber rock, and hints of classical, like Tegan and Sara, Chantal Kreviazuk, Melanie Doane, and Sarah Harmer. McLachlan defied description, and that lured multiple audiences to her music. She wrote songs that resonated in profound ways but were also relatable, and she inspired countless young women to believe that art

3 Beverly Keel, "Sexist 'Tomato' Barb Launches Food Fight on Music Row," *Tennessean*, May 27, 2015, https://www.tennessean.com/story/entertainment/music/2015/05/27/sexist-tomato-barb-launches-food-fight-music-row/28036657/.

4 Gerri Hirshey, "The Nineties," *Rolling Stone*, November 13, 1997.

made on their own terms wasn't just attainable but that it mattered and deserved to take up a festival's worth of space.

***

When McLachlan moved from Halifax to Vancouver in 1987, Terry McBride had big plans for her future. The Nettwerk Records co-founder had been circling her since he first heard McLachlan sing when she was just sixteen years old. He waited until she was nineteen to convince her to move to the other side of the country and pursue a solo career under his guidance.

Both *Touch*, her 1988 debut, and 1991's *Solace* made small waves in the indie community. But it was *Fumbling Towards Ecstasy* that established McLachlan's vision with total clarity. Every aspect of *FTE*, even down to its title, is an artsy teen's dream: grown-up in its sexuality but still awkward; poetic yet plainspoken. From the first track, "Possession," the mood is sensual and haunted, classy yet dangerous. In fact, it's far more sexual than I recall, but that's likely what attracted me to the song originally. It's mature and more subversive than the beauty of her voice suggests. It felt subversive to have McLachlan's church bell tower soprano singing about longing, desire, and darkness.

"Wait" paints a similar canvas: walking the knife's edge between beautiful and sinister, regretful and lustful. The words are lyrical and poetic, the phrasing sparse yet complicated as she sings about a shared dream to hold something precious together. There are hints that the song could be about abortion, or maybe even adoption — or was it just the fallacy of idealism and youth? When McLachlan sings about how leaving doesn't negate her love, how she's just not capable of more in this moment, it's devastating, packed with yearning, and still rooted in a remote, chilly space.

"Plenty" shares a bit of background vocal with Paula Cole's future hit "Where Have All the Cowboys Gone?," but when it shifts, the entire song soars. The lyrics continue to astound with their astute and unflinching truths about the hope that blooms in the lies we tell ourselves and the shattering aftermath of betrayal.

"Good Enough" is one of my favourites. It explores that fine line between self-esteem and self-destruction that comes from spending the night drinking and oversharing to the person next to you at the bar, a desperate yet hazy intimacy fostered in an exchange of confessions and the ways in which alcohol can sometimes strip the bullshit from our words and leave a stark, naked truth behind. What comes next in the song is a purposeful shift into something much deeper. It's gutting as McLachlan implores the object of this verse to leave an abusive partner, and there's a queer coding to the chorus if we read McLachlan as the narrator, advocating for herself as someone to trust, someone who wants to show them why they're more than, as the title says, "good enough." It's a hell of a complicated song that's also beautiful, important, and a small nod to McLachlan's burgeoning 2SLGBTQIA+ fan base.

"Mary" continues McLachlan's experimentation with religious iconography and highlights the stories of biblical women, giving voice and depth to characters who are too often relegated to being in service of men. It's a quiet number, with a steady, shuffling backbeat, and there's so much restraint, it almost feels like relief when McLachlan lets herself climb into the upper reaches of her soprano, gives up that control a bit as the chorus swells.

"Elsewhere" is another brilliant skyscraper of a song, even if the actual music and vocal delivery are somewhat monotone. It works in tandem with the subject matter, which explores choice and the necessary stubborn defiance of growing up. From friends hating your new partner to negotiating adulthood with one's parents, asserting one's identity for the first time is a fraught experience, and McLachlan gives it its due. "Circle," the album's weakest song, is still excellent lyrically, but the musical arrangement, which emphasizes a tougher, funkier sound, doesn't quite work. What I like about McLachlan's approach to love in contrast to Céline Dion's is that she explores all aspects of love — romantic, familial, and platonic — and not just the glorious highs and tragic lows, but the nuances, like how sometimes it keeps us committed to things that suck.

"Ice" is another high point of the record. The arrangement and delivery is appropriately atmospheric and wintery; the lyrics, a further testament to McLachlan's love of complicated language and biblical allusions. She references jilted-tongued angels and serpents, lying lovers, and an endless appetite for the bare minimum. It's an extraordinary song that again explores struggle, self-esteem, and identity using evocative imagery.

"Hold On" is, arguably, the record's best track, and McLachlan kicks the song off with a warning about the pain and discomfort to come. It's so perfect that I wish the album's sequencing had been different. This would easily tie, if not usurp, *Jagged Little Pill*'s opening and pointed question. "Hold On" taps every vein. Every word resonates and the momentum builds like a never-ending funicular climbing up into the clouds, raising the tension and the stakes until its sudden, abrupt conclusion.

It creates a free-fall effect, which is softened by "Ice Cream," almost a novelty song compared to the rest of the album, which nonetheless became a fan favourite. It's semi-sweet, fun, but not inconsequential, which is critical to its success. It has the most jazz influence of any of the songs, and it's upbeat despite lyrics that twist back and forth between hopeful and ominous, creating a welcome hint of tension.

The levity is short-lived and gives way to "Fear," a gutsy, strange, quintessentially '90s experience. The electronic influences and the string section are a fascinating juxtaposition to the ethereal choral vocal performance. There's pleasure in the pain as McLachlan scales her towering soprano and sings about fear, loss, loneliness, and intimate panic.

The title track, "Fumbling Towards Ecstasy," is the ideal finale for the record. McLachlan finds a resting place to lay all the themes out on the table — not necessarily a resolution, but a place to take a break from all the struggle. She promises to let go and be free, to love and rage without fear or constraint. It's a slow burn of a song that lives in the time after midnight when the candles come out and we're really at peace with ourselves, or perhaps we've simply confused peace with resignation and weary acquiescence.

McLachlan was a hugely empowering artist for me and so many of my friends. She inspired me to write, spurred others to pick up the guitar, and still others to sit down at the piano. She inspired us to find and articulate our own voices simply by utilizing hers. Not all girls need to see it to be it; I don't think I ever did simply because mine was a house without any kind of gendered competition — girls did what boys did, daughters did what their fathers did, no question — but many girls do need permission to flex and stretch into their own spaces. And all people benefit from representation, the normalization of seeing a variety of people occupying both basic and vaunted spaces.

***

With its very literal title, *Surfacing*, the follow-up to *Fumbling Towards Ecstasy*, warned us what it would be: McLachlan emerging from the depths, coming up for air. *Fumbling* peaked at #50 on the Billboard Hot 200 chart, whereas *Surfacing* peaked at #2. Of course, it's a record that more people could readily connect with than *Fumbling*: there's something triumphant about it — even as it tackles infidelity and disappointment, love and all its complications — and it's not entrenched in the murky complexity of identity the way *Fumbling* was.

Critics weren't always kind to McLachlan, including *Entertainment Weekly*'s Jim Farber, who, in his review of *Surfacing* says, "McLachlan sings like an angel and writes like a wretch. In a voice both shimmering and omniscient, she expresses a ruinous enslavement to love."[5] In the review, he says she "pants" and "mewls" and describes her soul as "enfeebled." But if it sounds negative, perhaps Farber's just fronting for the guys, because he ultimately decides her recordings have never sounded more dense or alive, though he credits that to producer Pierre Marchand and mentor Daniel Lanois.

When *Surfacing* was released in 1997, expectations were huge. The album was a commercial success (it's McLachlan's

5 Jim Farber, "Surfacing," *Entertainment Weekly*, July 25, 1997.

best-selling record to date), but it was a disappointment to me. I wasn't interested in how she wanted to evolve as an artist, and that's my problem. It's a bolder, more confident pop record, but compared to *Fumbling*, it feels flat — squashed by too much production and lyrically much more restrained. At times it felt uninspired, or as if some hit-maker songwriter showed up and insisted everybody follow a certain formula for next-level stardom. If that was the case, it worked, though I think it's worth examining at what cost to the integrity of the art.

Despite the new direction, there is still plenty of McLachlan's personality present on the first track, "Building a Mystery." But even with the description of a man as "beautiful" and "fucked up," the song still feels safer than anything in *Fumbling Towards Ecstasy*. Lyrically, the repetition is too overt to be effective, which not only dilutes the song's impact but infects every track on the record. "I Love You" is the first clear indication that this was not the McLachlan I'd fallen for originally. Love songs can be amazing, but lyrically this feels like something from a pile of Dion's rejects as McLachlan sings about an island of hope, shared breath, and anguished longing. It's overly mannered, overwritten, and overwrought. The arrangement does it no favours, either: ghostly and whispery, like a shimmery sky full of falling stars that end up smothering us all to death.

"Adia" is likely the best song on the record in terms of production and structure, but it's the least ambitious lyrically, which still strikes me as weird given the gossip about the song's scandalous source material. Allegedly it is about McLachlan acknowledging her affair with her drummer, Ashwin Sood, who was her friend's partner. "Adia" bandies about concepts of innocence and falls from grace, and it seems to suggest that since everyone is flawed, do our indiscretions really matter? It's a total non-apology that talks in abstracts rather than concretes, which is emblematic of much of *Surfacing*'s lyrical content.

"Do What You Have to Do" is another impossible knot of justification, guilt, and defensiveness, which might be why it's so stiffly written. McLachlan is hugely capable of elegant, interesting, intellectual lyrics; here every song feels like words used as a coat of armour. It's almost pretentious, but I think it's ultimately more about trying to write from inside a situation and protect one's self.

"Witness" is the song that finally leads the listener to a place that feels good, not awkward. It's plaintive, humble, and honest. Lyrically it's much simpler than some of the other tracks on the album. It's less fussy, which makes it much more impactful, even as it revisits concepts of forgiveness, failure, and atonement. A guitar solo comes out of nowhere, and it's a great, wrenching moment that heightens the tension and angst of the song.

"Black and White" is a strange detour into an almost samba-esque beat and it should be on a Holly Cole record, not Sarah McLachlan's. It could be a genuinely great song, but Sood's drums are pushed into the spotlight and it's a terrible juxtaposition with McLachlan's vocals. The drums are routinely the weakest part of the whole record, and yet there they are, jockeying to share the spotlight. It's a rambling sort of song; at least the repetition here serves its purpose as the song fades out to its haunting conclusion.

"Full of Grace" is by far my favourite song on the record, and that's because it's the least *Surfacing*-like song, since it's a carry-over from *Rarities, B-Sides & Other Stuff*. Coupled with the final track, the record's end is like a warm, full-body embrace.

"Last Dance," entirely composed of piano, strings, and saw, is simple and devastating. It's a weird, wonderful, and daring way to close out a radio-friendly record, and it warms my heart even now, because it takes guts to end an album with a two-minute instrumental. After all of the disappointment I had felt in *Surfacing*'s midsection, there was some comfort in these last two songs, like hands clasping mine, an old friend returned. The last track in particular felt like a secret high-five from the McLachlan I worshipped so completely, and I was grateful for it.

★★★

Rarities, B-Sides & Other Stuff came out in 1996, and sonically it's something of a critical bridge between *Fumbling* and *Surfacing*. I suppose I didn't really forget about it, not really, but I hadn't intended to write about it originally. I loved it and was obsessed with it, but I hadn't listened to it in forever. Turns out there was a reason why I'd let myself get some distance from it.

Listening now, there's a rawness to *Rarities* that's largely absent from *Surfacing*. "Dear God" is everything I love about McLachlan: sassy, provocative, and just toeing the line of sacrilegious. Written by XTC's Andy Partridge, it's a scathing indictment, and yet McLachlan balances it by making clear how much her anger comes from a place of deep concern. It's a thrill to hear McLachlan raise these kinds of questions, and it still feels bold now considering how frightened people are of truly challenging the very existence of God. The ferocity is reminiscent of the late Sinéad O'Connor, and it's great.

Given the huge success of McLachlan's 1995 single "I Will Remember You," made famous that same year in the film *The*

Brothers McMullen, *Rarities'* best trick is the sequencing: following up "Dear God" with "I Will Remember You" ensured most people couldn't ignore "Dear God," even if they wanted to. I love that. I also love "I Will Remember You," despite its ubiquity as a funeral staple, which has made it a pop culture joke at this point. The song sticks to your skin and seeps into your bones, but it's not just about this one song. It's this sequence that is triggering. There is so much loss and pain and sorrow. And suddenly, just like that, I'm inside my grief, quietly back beside my father's dead body and I don't even fully understand why, except I'm struck by how cliché this is. In fact, this is where I started crying in a coffee shop and hid behind a curtain of my hair so my friend working beside me wouldn't notice.

"Gloomy Sunday" features McLachlan's soaring soprano in full effect again, and the song lives up to its name. I had to stop the song and just close my eyes and cry, quietly, while a bunch of memories came flooding back to me. I kept writing, kept writing, kept writing, because that's what you do. What follows is almost exactly as I wrote it in that moment:

> What does it say about me that I didn't let myself acknowledge that I pitched a book with a time frame that encapsulated my father's death until right at this moment, listening to *Rarities, B-Sides & Other Stuff*, and started crying at "I Will Remember You" and then fully lost it at "Gloomy Sunday"? I remember losing myself in this record after my father died, trying to find some kind of solace in the fact that I was still alive but my life was over, or at least the life I'd always known.

There's nothing that feels as comparable, I don't think, when you're a kid, because your parents are always just supposed to be there; they are supposed to be people you can take for granted and depend on and are rooted to, forever, and it's so unfathomable that you can be seventeen and suddenly be an orphan. Intellectually you understand it, but you don't know how it feels until it happens to you.

Jesus. What do I keep buried inside me that I didn't fully admit what I was doing, what I was writing, at least in part, until this moment, now, in the midst of writing, when I saved Sarah for last, when I had totally all but forgotten *Rarities* and didn't think about it, didn't feel it 'til now.

I've heard these songs a million times in the last seventeen years and it doesn't take me back every time, but listening in this order, these songs sandwiched next to each other, the anger and sorrow and loss and loneliness. My body and my heart are both horrified and exhausted, hit by a train. I may legit be a little bit unhinged, still in denial, less than whole. Still less than whole. How, after all these years, is that possible?

I am an unreliable narrator. That's how we all survive, how we all cope. We keep pieces of ourselves as far away as possible, at least out of the forefront, though of course they're always there. Lies we tell ourselves to make living easier. This is kindness, actually, because that is how

> to deal with something. That is sometimes what dealing looks like. There are no other places to hide inside my head. This is it. This is where I find some kind of release, some kind of reckoning. This is where I begin to breathe again, fill up my lungs with clarity and try to shake myself from the paralyzing, numbing shock that I have been so committed to my delusions, or at least to my escapes, entrenched in my survival.

Dad died on December 17, 1996, six weeks shy of my eighteenth birthday, and the life that I knew was over. My known life had ended once before, too, when my mother left my father six years earlier, but that felt different. It hurt less somehow — a paper-cut versus an amputation. My parents' separation wasn't great, but it wasn't upending chaos. It wasn't free fall. But Dad dying was a hole in my chest, a shotgun blast through and through, an empty loneliness that I thought would fill up again. I didn't know I would just end up growing around it instead.

After my parents split up, my father bought a second-hand store called Jack's. It was massive, thousands of square feet stacked high with furniture and packed tight with boxes filled with random treasures and, yes, sometimes total crap. My sister and I spent huge chunks of our youth in that store and at his side. He worked long hours, hauling couches, dining room tables, and heavy wooden hutches to and from people's homes, building up and dismantling lives by request. We joined him, spending long stretches of summer weekends and weeknights combing through yard sales and estate sales, setting up our space at the flea market, being grown-ups.

He was Bob. A newspaper once used the phrase "Bob beamed" to describe him and he liked that, because for the most part he was funny and friendly and easygoing. He was a large man, with thick dark hair, sometimes bearded and sometimes not. He enjoyed our reactions when he would disappear into the bathroom for a long time and suddenly come out clean-shaven and unrecognizable. He was an anchor in our lives, a man with two daughters and a mother (my grandmother), who actively helped raise us from the time I was two. He was always there, even if he was working late and getting up early. Dad was there.

And then suddenly he wasn't. He caught a virus, it developed into pneumonia, and he was stubborn. He kept working. One day he was barely conscious. I convinced him to go to the hospital — I would run the store that Sunday, it would be fine. I dropped him off at the hospital in New Westminster and went back later that night. I honestly don't remember much of the specifics after that, but I believe he was so sick that he was already depriving his organs of oxygen. Our lives became a vigil. Less than two weeks later, he was dead.

As I mentioned, it's impossible to predict the places grief will take you; it's also impossible to predict the places it forces you to go. Mine directed me into this book, and just like McLachlan's music, it continues to reveal new truths to me decades later.

Rarities was my refuge, and following the trigger of "Gloomy Sunday," there's a gentle, sad warmth in "Full of Grace." It's a welcome respite. There's hope in the strings that swell gently behind McLachlan's gorgeous vocals. There's hope in the grace she extends to herself and to all of us who recognize ourselves in the song. As the lyrics repeat a similar theme of hers — apologizing and acknowledging that her current capacity for love isn't enough — there's hope in the wishing that things could be different.

"Song for a Winter's Night" takes Gordon Lightfoot's classic and turns it into a rich, dense, dreamy escape. The layers of vocals, the subtle drum, whispers of flute — it's a warm, cozy drink on a cold, cold night. "Blue," another incredible cover of a Canadian icon, Joni Mitchell, whom McLachlan has been compared to many, many times (a rite of passage if you're a Canadian woman who writes songs and plays a guitar), is short, simple, raw, and full of glorious harmonies and textures.

The sequencing of the record meant everything to me. *Rarities* was a map for my grief. Eventually it became the map that helped me out of my grief. Or so I thought. I've always known that grief is permanent, at least in some small way. It's not like I thought I'd healed completely or gotten over it. Of course not. I still cry randomly when I'm caught unawares or a chance memory sneaks up on me and sticks me in my side. I can't even make sense of the fact that I'm so much older now than my dad ever was; that as of this book's rerelease, I will be forty-five years old, and I will keep going (knock on wood) and that he will always be someone who died at thirty-nine.

He was so goddamned young. I'm grateful for the years I had with him, of course. I love the fact that I can think back on our life and see all the ways he still lives inside me today, how he helped me get to this moment, how he told me that writers need to show people their work, that writers need readers. He was private and proud, and hilarious and sharp, and his heart was generous and kind.

I left Vancouver for Victoria in the fall of 1997 to start university and leave behind all the upheaval at home. My sister, grandmother, and I had, after my father's death, moved in with my mother, her partner, and my uncle. We shared a house and it was the first time I'd ever had my own bedroom. I put six geographical hours between the rest of my family, my friends, and me to start something new that was mine alone. The highs and lows of that year were unlike anything I'd ever experienced before.

Sarah McLachlan factored into my new life, too. During my first few days of dorm living, I met my future BFF, J. Within a week of knowing each other, we decided to buy tickets to an upcoming McLachlan concert in Vancouver. When we went to buy our tickets, we decided to get tattoos — not matching, just in the same spot — to mark the beginning of our new lives as grown-ups. What's more grown-up than deciding to spend student loan money on something like a tattoo? It also marked the beginning of this new friendship that we both somehow knew would be important. (And it is. She's still my best friend today. Our relationship has survived our sometimes disparate tastes in music, and we're family.) That was also the year of Lilith Fair. It felt celebratory and important, but it took until I was writing about music professionally to fully grasp that Lilith Fair was basically a unicorn, a sasquatch, and an Oompa-Loompa all in one. It was weird, rare, and magic.

Consider that even in 2015, Coachella was casually referred to as "BroChella." According to *Slate*'s Dee Lockett, the festival, which started in 1999 (Lilith Fair's last year), had less than sixteen percent female-driven acts on its bill in 2015. In 2018, Beyoncé became just the third woman headliner ever in Coachella's twenty-year history. There had been 785 male headliners in that same time span.[6] An internet's worth of headlines have exposed similarly distressing numbers about gender inequality at summer festivals. Lilith Fair was entirely centred on women and women-fronted bands. People argued then that it was unnecessary, but they were wrong. If anything, we've never more desperately needed a Lilith-like festival, despite the fact that McLachlan and organizers tried and failed to resuscitate it in 2010. But a revamped Lilith Fair for today that centres trans and racialized women, gender variant, queer, and nonbinary folks? Yes, please!

The '90s were a remarkable decade that shaped girls like me and the people we would become. When you come of age in a time when women have voices and take up space as visible creators and entrepreneurs, it never dawns on you that silence is the rule and these women, your idols, are the exception.

Sarah McLachlan has been the quietest of the core four over the past decade. In 2016, she released *Wonderland*, a Christmas album, as well as a one-off single called "The Long Goodbye." It's a slow, measured, piano-forward pop song that seems to be about a man the narrator just can't quit, even though she knows she should. The resignation in her voice bleeds into the arrangement. McLachlan sounds beautiful but empty, and it's a bummer. I miss the emotional complexity and lyrical nuance that helped

6 Tobi Akingbade, "Beyonce Is Headlining Coachella 2018 but Why Is There Still a Gender Gap Issue at Festivals?" *Metro* (U.K.), April 14, 2018, https://metro.co.uk/2018/04/14/beyonce-headlining-coachella-2018-still-gender-gap-issue-festivals-7467543/.

transform her voice, that allowed her to transcend beauty for something singular and iconic. Consider McLachlan's cover of Joni Mitchell's "Blue," the haunting chill of her soprano and the urgent tumble of her lower register as her vocal range mimics the song's narrative roller coaster, the push and pull of something toxic and intoxicating, a love that calms and storms like the ocean. McLachlan first covered "Blue" on 1996's *Rarities, B-Sides & Other Stuff*. That album went triple platinum, and it's easily one of McLachlan's best, in part because of her interpretation of "Blue." Her version doesn't take from Mitchell's original, nor is it a karaoke imitation, but rather Mitchell's mastery seems to inspire McLachlan to stretch herself within the song and make it her own while still paying tribute to one of her musical heroes.

McLachlan actually performed "Blue" when Mitchell was awarded the Governor General's Performing Arts Award in Canada in 1996. Twenty-five years later, McLachlan joined Mitchell onstage for Mitchell's massive comeback show. Mitchell, who'd suffered a stroke years earlier, had all but disappeared from the public eye until Americana singer-songwriter and activist Brandi Carlile became friends with Mitchell and began encouraging her to start playing and singing again at home with friends. As these "Joni Jams" continued, Mitchell began teaching herself how to play guitar again by watching old videos of herself performing on YouTube. In 2022, Carlile and Mitchell staged a surprise appearance at Newport Folk Festival when Mitchell took to the stage and performed with a crowd of musicians all around her. This triumphant return to performing sparked another exciting announcement: Joni Mitchell's Joni Jam for one night only at the Gorge in Washington State. McLachlan's performance of "Blue" was among the evening's highlights.

I love when McLachlan surprises us, as she did with her 2020 feature on T. Thomason's "Bliss Pt. II." Thomason, a young singer-songwriter originally from Halifax, was partnered with McLachlan when he appeared on the reality TV singing competition show *The Launch*. McLachlan was one of his mentors, and the pair connected artistically. The following year, when Thomason decided to re-record his debut EP and reimagine the songs with other artists, McLachlan was his dream "get." "I've been a huge fan of Sarah's music for a long time and thought this could be a wicked fit musically," Thomason shared. "But getting to know her a little bit in the last couple of years and seeing the relationships she has with her daughters and lifelong friends was really what catapulted this collab into my mind. 'Bliss' is precious to me, and the only way I could imagine reimagining it was if it felt right all the way down to the bones."[7]

In a 2018 interview, Thomason talked about the importance of finding inclusive collaborators within the music industry as a nonbinary trans person and noted his privilege as someone who now passed as a "young, slim, white dude or binary-trans dude, most of the time. So, I think that's meant I've missed out on a lot of bullshit that many other nonbinary and trans folks face. I will say that it was a very eye-opening experience to observe who was able to handle my transition gracefully within the music industry and who was not. People will surprise you in good and bad ways."[8]

---

7 "Interview: T. Thomason Talks New Song 'Bliss Part II' w/ Sarah McLachlan, What He'd Tell His Younger Self, Advice for Queer Creators + More," *Soundzine*, October 7, 2020, http://www.soundzine.ca/2020/10/interview-t-thomason-talks-new-song.html.

8 Bee Delores, "Essay: What It's Like to Be a Non-Binary Musician," *B-Sides & Badlands*, https://bsidesbadlands.com/rae-spoon-shawnee-t-thomason-non-binary-interview-essay/.

McLachlan is one of the people who has shown up for Thomason. She talked about meeting him on *The Launch* and being "immediately drawn to his humility and artistry." McLachlan said she was thrilled when he asked her to help him reimagine "Bliss," which she called a "hauntingly simple ode to self-discovery and resilience . . . T. has a deep emotional connection to the songs he writes and a soul-baring truth to his performances and I'm so proud of what he's accomplished with 'Bliss Part II.'"[9]

Championing younger musicians and amplifying their art with her sizable microphone and spotlight is a natural extension of McLachlan's already well-established legacy with her long-running music school. And, of course, Lilith Fair literally changed the music industry — at least for a little while — and disrupted the patriarchal and sexist status quo. The festival's effects didn't seem long-lasting at the time, but McLachlan and co. planted a hell of a lot of seeds that have been bearing fruit the last several years. With a more radical, diverse, and inclusive reimagining, Lilith Fair 3.0 could be closer than we think.

9 "Interview: T. Thomason Talks."

THE '90S

When Girls Ruled, Fools Drooled, and Lilith Fair Levelled the Playing Field

As a teen, I was mad a lot — fiery, maybe. I was constantly embattled and arguing and fighting about or for something. I didn't fully realize this about myself until I started to dig deeper and scrape away at my childhood to reveal the hidden map of how I came to be a feminist. I reached for moments, specific and decisive anecdotes, but grasped at air and hazy memories. I have a terrible memory for most things; instead I have a general feelings bank of loose recollections and emotional and intellectual triggers to fall back on.

I asked my grandmother if there were any specifics I'd forgotten. "I'm trying to remember," I explained, "about how I became a feminist. But wasn't I always just like this?"

She thought for a few minutes, combing back through the decades.

"Yes."

She said I was always upset about inequality. It started when I was a little kid, with my schoolmate, S, who lived down the street. S was a good kid, well-behaved, polite, and pretty, but her mother put her down all the time. Her little brother, T, was a monster, but he could do no wrong. S's mother worshipped him. She also spent an inordinate amount of time praising my sister and me — our fair skin, our intelligence. But it was never just a compliment to us; every word came at the expense of her daughter. She was ugly, dumb, a stupid girl. My sister and I were wonderful. T was a tiny god in a six-year-old's body. It wasn't fair.

I found this attitude repeated in various ways, sometimes subtly and other times implicitly, throughout a diverse cross-section of homes in our little neighbourhood. There were very few houses where equality had a seat at the dinner table. Cultural and religious norms took precedent, old-school values were staunchly passed on as familial inheritance, and I found myself inspired to willfully subvert any situation wherein girls were made to feel they were less than. Like being ignored or diminished in favour of male siblings, or forced to be servile to parents and family because "that's what girls are for," or generally denied any agency, bound by anything where their desires or thoughts or dreams were deemed inessential.

Artists like Céline Dion and Shania Twain had a voice and a platform, their wants and desires and thoughts were deemed essential by millions of fans, and that made me even angrier. They appeared to be wasting every opportunity available to be advocates for something I categorized as better / stronger / bolder. In their music, they seemed to prioritize traditional gender roles and stereotypes. I didn't want to see myself in the people who liked Dion's and Twain's music. I thought I was better and more evolved than them. It's probably the ugliest part about me, the part that I've worked hardest to shed as an adult: the need to feel superior — artsier, cooler, smarter, tougher — to the people who loved me. Dion's and Twain's fans must have been petty and small, otherwise how could they find meaningful escape in that music and those images? Clearly they were willfully ignorant and far too easily conned into falling in line with the status quo. They were sheep who didn't challenge life enough, whereas I relished the idea of myself as a lone wolf: rebellious and unique. Ugh. I was wildly pretentious. Fifteen is fifteen is fifteen, but it's kind of hard to look at and confront even decades later.

Adding up the plot points to one light bulb moment isn't really the way an identity works, even though I was trying to figure out what made me the person I am. We don't realize what sticks to us, how moments shape us, until after the fact, if we ever really do. Feminism, however, was, for me, always the answer.

My family wasn't a churchgoing one, but I went once when I was five or so and again when I was fourteen. Both times, a minister or some old white dude stood at the front of the room and talked loudly about who did and did not deserve to stand in God's light. The men went on and on about how people like us, regular folks, had to kneel down and do all of these demeaning things to be worthy. I never bought it. It sounded abusive and controlling and not at all like something I ever wanted to be involved in. These early, patriarchal, and crappy examples of religion had me convinced that almost all organized religion was toxic. I didn't see the non-toxic, community-based, and inclusive elements possible in religious community until well into my twenties.

One of my high school friends, also named S, was very religious, but this didn't really get in the way of our closeness. We argued about theological things, and what I deemed the patriarchal side of both her church and her home. Her parents were lovely people, but her father worked and handled everything; her mother, a gentle, smiling woman, minded the children but seemed to handle nothing, or at least have no say in any aspect of the household or family life. No bills, no grocery shopping, no money, nothing. When my friend's father died suddenly, her mother was left untethered. My friend had to do everything: work out finances, budget, shop, pay bills, file paperwork, help raise her brother, and take care of her mother. It broke my heart, but it also infuriated me. Her father had controlled everything, his wife was never his equal, and now that dynamic managed to rob my friend of her adolescence. My friend, a singer, had loved Céline Dion, but as she moved into this unwelcome role of head of the household, she grew to love Sarah McLachlan more. Inspired by McLachlan, she picked up a guitar. Moved by her grief, she picked up a pen, and we spent hours in her candlelit bedroom, her playing McLachlan covers, then Morissette covers, and then her own original compositions.

Three years later, after my own father's death, McLachlan and Morissette bonded me still further to that friend. My grief also bonded me to a boy that I thought I loved. But at the same time, it isolated me from my best friend, M. We had already been drifting apart for a few years, and my choices, the way that I expressed grief and whom I sought comfort in, pushed us to our breaking point. It was messy as hell, spectacular in the way only teenagers can have a falling-out that doesn't result in murder: tears, betrayal, epic fighting. The aftershocks took out our whole group of friends, splintering everybody into factions. I had guessed this was coming. I'd read enough young adult books to realize there was a reason no series ever continued into college, but I figured it would happen after graduation and devolve a little more naturally. I had never imagined it would involve my father dying and a grief circle sparking jealous recriminations and emotional reckonings, as well as multiple different inseparable duos who weren't us also breaking in half.

But the reason I suspected it was coming — totally seriously — was M's love of Shania Twain. I knew that was the beginning of the end. Looking back now, I can see how much more of a role I played in our subsequent bust-up than I originally believed. I loved her, she was my friend, but her love for Twain absolutely gave me pause. In fact, we fought about it and not infrequently. I found M increasingly boy crazy and desperate to be popular. She probably found me bitchy and confoundingly desperate for the love of a boy she considered a total loser. Even before Dad died, M and I were already starting to come apart. If we'd been taught that some things aren't forever, maybe it wouldn't have been so disastrous, but we were BFFs. It was right there in the title. So instead of recognizing that our interests were changing and respecting those differences, we took each new personality facet as a slap in the face. Or at least I did.

M's love of Shania Twain wasn't simply her choice; it was a personal attack and an indication that she wasn't who she used to be. The thing is, that's always who she was. I was just an idiot who hated Twain. I was so convinced that I was right and Twain was wrong that it became a kind of permission for me to start pulling away or at least putting some distance between me and M. I couldn't relate to her anymore, or at least I felt I couldn't, and I chose to seek solace in other people when my father died. Specifically other people who shunned Twain and shared my preferred emotional and musical refuge of Morissette and McLachlan.

How narrow-minded was that?

Well, it was and it wasn't. Music was everything to me, and even though I wasn't fully aware of its prominence in my life then, I let it call the shots and guide my decisions in ways that are still revealing themselves to me now, even though I've been writing about music for years. Unpacking one's life, song by song, album by album, is, of course, just one way to look back. Music is both passive and active, a mutable and shape-shifting sort of art that cements moments and untethers others in equal measure. Predicting the limitations of a friendship based on what music each party likes and/or doesn't like makes some sense if music is more than entertainment. If music represents something bigger and more substantial, and has become the vital component of one's identity, it's easy to take two seemingly incompatible things and extrapolate ruin.

But it's also an easy way out, a subconsciously cowardly justification or a less invasive means of parsing more complicated, deeper feelings that we aren't usually given the tools to dismantle ourselves. Again, it's that endlessly problematic concept of "love = forever." Sometimes I think it's even more important and vital to our development to explore the damage that does on platonic relationships rather than romantic ones. In my experience, there are few things as intense/all-consuming/rewarding/co-dependent/joyous/damaging as the dizzying attachment of girls in BFF relationships.

Breakups between BFFs feel like a holy trifecta of loss: death, being separated from a conjoined twin, and a broken heart. Friend breakups are devastating under the best circumstances, but when combined with other major life changes, teenage hormones, and the collateral damage of entire friend hives imploding, the ramifications are endless. Twain didn't ruin M and me — I did. It was ugly because I didn't know any other way for it to be. In 1997, I was chest-deep in aching grief and heartbreak over my father's death, and he was the one "good" father in my whole circle of friends: present, reliable, stable, strong. His death was a vacuum in all our lives. I found no comfort with M.

Instead, I wanted to be inside a shared grief with another friend whose father had died a few years earlier. S knew what survival looked like; she knew the starkness of a totally different and unfathomable future. I wanted to be with the boy I secretly loved, even though he didn't love me back the way I wanted. I was happy to take whatever affection he had to give, to lay with him on my bed, pressed up tight together, crying into his shoulder, his arms hugging me, feeling both safe and intimate and undone in a way I'd never known. His mouth found my mouth, and everything made sense. It was urgent and emotional and it meant everything and nothing, though I wouldn't know that for a few more years. M and I stopped speaking in the summer of 1997 and didn't talk again for ten years.

We eventually found our way back to each other and the credit goes entirely to M for that. We're friends again, and though we don't see each other too often, I'm grateful to have her back in my life. I see now that it didn't have to be Twain or McLachlan, or Dion or Morissette. Those were divisions I made, and though those particular distinctions didn't disappear without some time and critical thinking on my part over the years, 1997 did introduce a slightly more cohesive concept of solidarity into my life.

***

I was always sort of a shit disturber, in a very politically minded students' rights way. I believed that my voice could matter, that every teenager's and young person's voice had value, but high school has a way of silencing and squashing attempts at radicalism. In Grade 10, I helped start a high school newspaper that was banned by our second issue, thanks in part to an editorial I'd written criticizing (okay, trashing) the new career preparation curriculum, which presumed all students could find places for themselves in a few very narrow fields of interest, and that most high school students weren't already working. (The school board wouldn't give credit for actually having a job already.) Growing up in East Vancouver, lots of us were working by the time we were sixteen years old, if not earlier.

I've liked the fight ever since my elementary school principal abolished the student government (I was the president) and cancelled our Grade 7 graduation dance. A few of my schoolmates, our parents, and I fundraised and held our graduation dance on our own — ditching school for the afternoon — across the field at the community centre gym fifty metres away. It was my first taste of grassroots protest and success, and it was amazing. It was like *Footloose* without the slut-shaming and domestic violence.

By high school, I learned that most of my peers were unlikely to fight for something better for a variety of reasons: they didn't know how, they didn't think they deserved better, or they never realized fighting was an option. But I liked a fight, and it wasn't enough to just manipulate a situation to work for me that didn't also serve the greater good. Thus, my high school editorial calling for alternative career preparation experiences that were actually related to our future fields of study, and thus my quick lesson in censorship. When I fought the newspaper ban, my guidance counsellor mistook my tears for gendered weakness; he deemed me "too emotional" to be reasonable. I was rage-crying, nothing more, and his sexist attitude only made me want to rage-cry more. If I didn't channel my feelings into angry tears, I would probably have a criminal record by now. Tears are "too emotional," "too girly," or "too unreasonable." Bullshit. Sometimes I cry so that I don't rip a dude's throat out.

That interaction forged something inside me, as did another, more traumatizing experience that while small, should probably include a trigger warning for a description of sexual assault in the next four paragraphs.

My feminism became activism in some small way after my first Take Back the Night rally, a then-annual march against gendered violence. I had friends who had been sexually assaulted, and it was devastating. Empowered, maybe, by the pop culture hints and explicit confessions of Morissette and McLachlan and artists like Tori Amos, Take Back the Night (and its demands to make the streets safe for women at any time) made its way onto my radar in Grade 10. I don't remember exactly how I got there, but I remember the strange invincibility of being in a huge crowd of women, all demanding one thing: that we be safe on our own streets. My own experiences were small, and seemed almost inconsequential by comparison, but I still felt foolish for not recognizing what they were sooner.

Almost anywhere in the world, if you get up early enough and you're an old man, you can find another random group of old men drinking coffee somewhere. When my grandfather came to visit, he went to the McDonald's a few blocks from our apartment. My sister and I sometimes went with him.

After he died, when we saw various members of that group, we'd say hello or share a laugh. Some of the old men were definitely . . . well, characters is probably the best word to describe them. Ol' Toothless was one of them, but he was harmless. Pokey-Pokey Man was different. He was grizzled and grumpy and whenever I saw him he would poke my shoulder, but we never spoke. The nickname wasn't very clever. Eventually his poking drifted further down. I didn't think much of it at first, but soon I came to realize that he was poking me where he guessed my boobs were.

I was ashamed, and I felt totally stupid, and I freaked out. I was fourteen or fifteen at the time; I should have known better. I should have confronted him. I should have, should have, should have. When I told my father, he was furious: at himself, at the old man, and it felt like at me, though I realized later on that wasn't the case. He just felt helpless, like he'd failed somehow to protect me. I remember him asking, yelling, "Well, what do you want me to do? Go and punch him? Go and punch an old man?" I didn't want that. He wanted to, but mostly we both wanted the same thing: for it never to have happened in the first place. I remember looking at him and his useless anger and realizing for the first time that he didn't know how to fix it. I had to take part of the blame in that moment because he had nowhere else to put it. But I won't lie, I would have liked to have heard "it's not your fault." It was, in retrospect, the only time my father had even slightly let me down.

Music was my refuge. I felt vulnerable and naive, and I was grateful when *Jagged Little Pill* came along. It was a place to take cover and recharge, reassess my culpability and capabilities. Alanis Morissette made me fierce again, restored my outrage, and sped up my catharsis. Sarah McLachlan moved me through the grief that was ahead. Lilith Fair solidified my stance and backed me up.

***

The '90s began with Queen Latifah, Salt-N-Pepa, and Riot Grrrl and closed with Lilith Fair, Destiny's Child, and the Spice Girls. But in between, in addition to Dion, Twain, Morissette, and McLachlan, there was a vibrant scene of women indie rockers, electronic acts, punk bands, singer-songwriters, hip hop artists, pop groups, soul and R&B artists, and independent multi-genre musicians toiling in all corners of the country. They were unstoppable, inspiring, powerful women, and plenty of them found a home on the Lilith Fair circuit. Some would evolve into huge, international stars years later (hey, hey, Tegan and Sara), but all of them deserved to move out of the shadows and into the spotlight.

Somehow, Riot Grrrl had passed me by — it didn't really touch my life until years later — but I had Lilith Fair. My first Lilith Fair wasn't just inspiring; it was life-affirming. It validated me as a young woman. I didn't want to be onstage — that was never my thing — but I wanted to write and tell stories. I wanted to know that my voice had a place and that my words mattered, and Lilith Fair felt like one of the first places where those things were possible.

I was always a feminist, even if I didn't fully have the intricacies of the language down. I was inclined to surround myself with music made by women, artists like Morissette, McLachlan, Jann Arden, Hole, Melissa Etheridge, Deborah Cox, Liz Phair, Garbage, the Fugees and Lauryn Hill, and Fiona Apple. I wanted to fight sexism, and the best way I could think of doing that was to drown myself in women's voices — writers, authors, music, whatever. From 1993 to 1997, it seemed like the music industry was on my side. I wasn't terribly aware of the structural and, again, arbitrary barriers facing women musicians at the time, but I love that Lilith Fair began because someone dared to tell McLachlan that two women on the same bill would never work. When she looked around in 1996 and noticed that Lollapalooza's lineup featured zero women but that she "couldn't possibly" book a show with herself and one other woman, she channelled her frustration and her experience into creating Lilith Fair, the ultimate middle finger to the music industry's rampant and systemic sexism and misogyny.

The first Lilith Fairs were unofficial: four women-only lineups in four different cities featuring McLachlan and some of her friends. One of the proto Liliths was McLachlan's 1996 hometown show in Vancouver featuring Paula Cole and Lisa Loeb. The following year, Lilith Fair kicked off officially with a thirty-five-city summer tour and a host of high-profile and fledgling acts, all women solo artists or women-fronted bands. The tour grossed $16 million in ticket sales that first summer, and a success story was born.

I loved Lilith Fair. I didn't go to a lot of concerts as a teenager because there just wasn't enough money. But Lilith Fair was different. I really only remember the sets of three artists, specifically, from that day: Lisa Loeb, Indigo Girls, and Sarah McLachlan. But I will never forget the feeling of twenty-two thousand people together celebrating music made by women, people who understood it as art and not just women in music. It seems like semantics, but I think there's a key difference in how we frame the language of talking about music and gender. When we specify "woman guitarist" or "girl band," the implication is that women are Others and that music is, by default, a wholly male space except when infiltrated by a select few. Lilith Fair grew in response to an industry rooted in sexism and hypocrisy, an industry where women were deemed interlopers and outsiders, even as they saved it with millions and millions of record sales. In 1997, McLachlan told J.D. Considine of the *Baltimore Sun*:

> To say that there isn't sexism in the business is incredibly naïve. I've been very lucky, because I've had not much to do with it. But I know it exists. When I first put out 'Fumbling Towards Ecstasy' three years ago, there was this total competition between me and Tori Amos. It had nothing to do with us — it was totally to do with the radio stations and record companies pitting us against each other. Because there was this thing at radio stations, where they would say, "Well, we added Tori this week, so we can't add you." It was very marginalizing. What are you saying? That we sounded alike? You would never say, "Oh, we added Nirvana this week, so we can't add Pearl Jam." It was really stupid. It was like people were living by these old rules, like they were resigned to them, or didn't even think about what was going on and how ludicrous it was.[1]

1 J.D. Considine, "Feminine Musique: The Lilith Fair Is an All-Woman Music Festival, and It Has Been Playing to Packed Houses While Other Festivals Face Empty Seats," *Baltimore Sun*, July 27, 1997, https://www.baltimoresun.com/1997/07/27/feminine-musique-the-lilith-fair-is-an-all-woman-music-festival-and-it-has-been-playing-to-packed-houses-while-other-festivals-face-empty-seats/.

During a roundtable discussion organized by *Entertainment Weekly* in 1997, McLachlan was joined by fellow Lilith Fair participants Sheryl Crow, Joan Osborne, and Fiona Apple. Writer Chris Willman opens the piece by saying that it's "not surprising" that Apple, the youngest musician at just nineteen, brought out the "maternal side of the other three." As a dialogue between the four women, it's interesting, particularly when they touch on sexism, which comes up frequently in the most casual ways:

> OSBORNE: [Turning to Crow] You had that dress, that Dolce & Gabbana thing on . . .
>
> CROW: I took a lot of crap for that. [The press said] "We can see your underwear." I kept saying "That's the way the dress is supposed to be!"
>
> APPLE: You got a lot of crap, but didn't Jewel get even more?
>
> OSBORNE: That's part of what these things are about, though . . . everyone watching all the famous people get up on stage and cutting them apart. It's like ritual sacrifice. [To McLachlan] I'm hoping you're gonna include some things like this on the Lilith tour.
>
> MCLACHLAN: I think we need to have some mud wrestling.

> OSBORNE: Definitely — mud wrestling, ceremonial floggings, some mass induction into goddess-worship cults, some ritual sacrifice of high-ranking military officials caught in adultery . . .

When the writer interjects to ask if Lilith Fair is a victory celebration, McLachlan refutes the notion: "I don't know if I'd call it a victory celebration. That would mean that someone else would be admitting defeat. And this is not about being better than something else. It's celebrating what we are — the fact that after centuries of women's voices and ideas being suppressed, we've finally come into a time where women can be heard and respected and loved for what they say. That's something worth celebrating."[2]

In a 1997 interview with *Rolling Stone*, Shirley Manson of Garbage had some incredibly interesting, if depressing, things to say about sexism, Alanis Morissette, and Lilith Fair. With her frank, sexual, cool-as-fuck attitude, Manson was a hero to me and many of my friends:

> *ROLLING STONE*: What were the assumptions about women in rock when you started out?
>
> MANSON: [Shrugs] Well, they're the same as they always were: You've got no brains, you have no talent, you don't understand music, you have nothing to bring to the equation. And it's all about

2 Chris Willman, *Entertainment Weekly*, July 11, 1997.

your hooters and what you've got between your legs. Any woman who's successful has fucked every guy under the sun, you know? I mean, what aren't the assumptions?

ROLLING STONE: Do you think things have changed significantly for women?

MANSON: As sad as it is, women have only played a major part, artist-wise, for the past two years since Alanis Morissette came in and her record blew open the doors of every single radio station and showed programmers that, yes, people are interested in hearing women sing and, yes, women have something fresh to say. Well, surprise, surprise! The industry hasn't changed one iota. It just sees a possibility of making money.

ROLLING STONE: And most of the executives are men.

MANSON: Always, always, always. I haven't come across one woman in the whole time I've been involved in the record industry who has been in a position of immense power. And it'll be interesting to see what radio programmers are going to be saying in six months' time — this is very pessimistic of me, but I get the feeling they'll say, "Bring me back my white rock dudes."

ROLLING STONE: Your thoughts on Lilith Fair, please.

MANSON: I think they only showed one side of who women are — it was this cozy, middle-class, we-all-love-each-other and share-a-view-of-the-world and let's-hold-hands-and-go-forth-unto-the-world and show-how-great-we-are thing. And there's a million other women who don't feel that Lilith said anything for them. There were almost no black artists — Missy Elliott is producing, she's writing, she's rapping, she's doing all this stuff. Why aren't there people like Lil' Kim? Where are all the black girls who have huge selling power and are kicking up the dust and making people look at women in a different way? That said, Lilith is important because there are women who really do need fellowship and support. Because not everyone is like me — a loudmouthed fucker.

ROLLING STONE: Is rock & roll more or less sexist than society at large?

MANSON: Exactly the same. A lot of discussions are curtailed when you walk in a room, for instance, because it's not fit for female ears. A lot of talk about sex and women and whatever — for some inexplicable reason, men think there's some kind of animal that lurks in them that doesn't in women.

In 1997, Lilith Fair was a pointed target for people who claimed that a "women-only" lineup was "male bashing." "The last thing I wanted to be associated with is a festival that is perceived as man bashing," country artist Mary Chapin Carpenter told the *New York Times*. "I joined up when I realized that Lilith isn't about that, but about providing an antidote to that whole Lollapalooza testosterone scene."[3] The insults and casual/deliberate sexism of the nicknames alone were something special: Estro Fest, Breastfest, Labia Love In, Lesbopalooza, Girlapalooza. When you rile the (mostly white) dude/douche populace, it's pretty much confirmation that you're doing something right, right? Sure, but that was somewhat cold comfort as McLachlan and other performers faced accusations masked as questions from radio DJs and a variety of media people asking, "Why do you hate men?"

Because *of course* if one wants to celebrate women, that means hating men. And the thirty to forty percent of men who composed Lilith Fair's audience were a self-loathing group of weak-willed girly-boys, right? There couldn't possibly be men who genuinely enjoyed music of all varieties from all people, the way that women did every time they bought a ticket to Edgefest or Warped Tour. (Also, for the record, let's acknowledge what a deep hold the gender binary had on the culture in North America in the '90s, and how in contemporary times we are moving beyond the binary and better for it.)

What really had angry dudes making their baby faces and crying sexism between 1993 and 1997 was the fact that change had arrived. Riot Grrrl had been a fringe movement, Alanis

---

3 Neal Karlen, "On Top of Pop, but Not with One Voice," *New York Times*, July 11, 1997, https://www.nytimes.com/1997/06/29/arts/on-top-of-pop-but-not-with-one-voice.html.

Morissette's *Jagged Little Pill* was a warning, and Lilith Fair took a particular kind of feminism mainstream. According to an annual survey by the Recording Industry Association of America, this resulted in a sea change for music consumers as women bought more music than men for the first time.[4] Consumer power was shifting in favour of a commercially vibrant time for women and Lilith Fair benefitted from being at the forefront.

★★★

Attending Lilith Fair as a teenager inspired Brandi Carlile to pick up a guitar and start writing songs. In 2010, she signed on as one of the mainstage artists for Lilith Fair's ill-fated return. In *Vanity Fair*'s sprawling 2019 oral history of Lilith Fair (in which I participated and am quoted), Carlile explained how it led to her starting Girls Just Wanna Weekend in 2018, a resort-based concert festival held in Mexico. "I had got thrown off of a really high-profile tour with an all-male band that I idolized. From a handful of promoters not wanting to put on the show if I was on it, because they wanted two male-fronted guitar-rock bands. I deserved to be there. It lit a fire under my ass like you would not believe. Like most people, I don't realize there is a problem until it hits close. I started to realize there are not enough women in live music getting booked on these festivals. They are not getting record deals. They are not getting played on the radio. They are in a situation where Lilith Fair is needed again."[5]

---

4 Alexandra Marks, "Women Dominate Music Sales," *Christian Science Monitor*, April 8, 1998, https://www.csmonitor.com/1998/0408/040898.us.us.2.html.

5 Hopper, with Geffen and Pelly, "Building a Mystery."

Girls Just Wanna Weekend is billed as a female-fronted festival and a concert vacation. The fifth iteration of the festival took place January 18–21, 2024, and previous headliners include Sheryl Crow, Margo Price, and Indigo Girls. When a social media user teased Carlile that she "just wanted to bring Lilith Fair back," Carlile replied: "I never actually left Lilith fair tbh . . . lol I just wake up every day and live inside it for my whole life. I'm still there with my sunburn and indigo girls ball cap."[6]

Carlile also helms an annual weekend concert series at the Gorge in Washington State called Echoes through the Canyon. For the fourth annual event in 2023, Carlile programmed three nights. The first featured Marcus Mumford and Allison Russell, and McLachlan joined Carlile onstage for a surprise appearance. They performed a powerful singalong of a McLachlan Lilith Fair staple, "Hold On." On Saturday, the Joni Jam took place with Joni Mitchell's triumphant return to the stage and McLachlan's aforementioned guest appearance performing her cover of Mitchell's classic "Blue." On Monday night, Carlile performed with her country supergroup, the Highwomen, with guest Tanya Tucker. In a lengthy feature entitled "Brandi Carlile's Phenomenal Weekend at the Gorge Showed Why We Don't Just Need Joni Mitchell Back, but Lilith Fair, Too," *Variety* made the case for resurrecting McLachlan's groundbreaking festival and quoted what Carlile told the audience on the second night:

> I saw all three Lilith Fairs, which changed everything about what I wanted my job to look like,

6 Brandi Carlile (@brandicarlile), "I never actually left Lilith fair tbh . . . ," X, June 16, 2023, 4:26 p.m., https://twitter.com/brandicarlile/status/1669803615375212544.

> what I wanted my life to look like. I wanted to be like Sarah and bring lots and lots of women together to make big, big, beautiful, powerful noises. Women *and* men, but I feel like we live in a time when the women need a little more platforming, especially as we age and we're no longer allowed to have that platforming. I think it's really, really important whenever we get one to just step up, give everybody a leg up and keep the door open as long and as hard as you can. And this stage has seen many powerful women walk across it and celebrate one another, with no competition and a spirit of kindness.[7]

Two Lilith Fair oral histories have been published in the last decade, one in *Glamour* in 2017[8] and the *Vanity Fair* piece in 2019.[9] To have two important legacy print magazines devote so much space to Lilith Fair, and to do so in a way that prioritizes the voices of an array of people — headliners, second- and third-stage artists, organizers, crew, journalists, and attendees — is a small miracle. By literally making a space for Lilith Fair, both publications made a case for the festival's importance. The interviews provide so much context for the hype, criticism, media

---

7 Chris Willman, "Brandi Carlile's Phenomenal Weekend at the Gorge Showed Why We Don't Just Need Joni Mitchell Back, but Lilith Fair, Too," *Variety*, June 14, 2023, https://variety.com/2023/music/concert-reviews/brandi-carlile-gorge-weekend-recap-canyon-joni-mitchell-jam-1235643813/.

8 Melissa Maerz, "The Oral History of Lilith Fair, as Told By the Women Who Lived It," *Glamour*, July 5, 2017, https://www.glamour.com/story/the-oral-history-of-lilith-fair.

9 Hopper, with Geffen and Pelly, "Building a Mystery."

fervour, community impact, and magnitude of Lilith Fair's influence, and they offer a chance for many of the people originally involved to counter some of the rampant sexism, misogyny, and gendered assumptions about its purpose. Lilith Fair didn't fuck around, and these oral histories remind us of its power.

But some of the criticism of Lilith Fair was glaringly valid then and remains so today. It was absolutely a celebration of women. But it was, as Shirley Manson told *Rolling Stone*, visibly a celebration of white women, especially in its first year. A win for white women is not a win for all women, but that is something that some Lilith Fair organizers and artists seemed unwilling or unable to address at the time or, even now, decades later. Since 1997, McLachlan has acknowledged the lack of diversity — racially and musically — of that first year with some variation of "we asked everyone, this is who said yes." But we've never heard her or her co-organizers take it a step further and own the fact that they did not have meaningful relationships with many racialized artists or their managers. They did not have any kind of community with historically oppressed or excluded artists, so there was no trust and no pre-existing collaborations. They were white people with a lot of power in the music industry who were looking to extract from racialized artists. They might ultimately also be amplifying those artists and exposing them to new audiences, but McLachlan and her Lilith Fair co-founders were the power holders and moneymakers and they have never, at least publicly, taken that next step in the process by acknowledging their privilege and that they could have, and should have, done more.

Based on McLachlan's own words, there's still little accountability with regards to Lilith Fair's lack of diversity. This is an excerpt from *Glamour* and features a quote from India.Arie.

> McLACHLAN: That was the thing we had to defend more than anything else, more than our feminism, more than our choice to have just women. It was: Why you don't have more black artists, more R&B artists, different kinds of music, representing everybody?
>
> ARIE: I know why they called it the white-chicks folk fest, but I love that music.
>
> McLACHLAN: I don't think Perry Farrell was taken to task for those things [when he put together Lollapalooza]. We were doing something that really hadn't been done before, so anytime there's anything new happening, there is the desire to tear it down or find holes. Especially if you're trying to do something good. It pisses people off.[10]

McLachlan's right that Farrell wasn't criticized for "those things," but that doesn't mean the criticism directed at her and her co-founders wasn't valid. Pointing out inherent racial bias is not "finding" holes. The holes exist, and no amount of attempted gaslighting will prove otherwise. Terry McBride, Lilith Fair co-founder and owner of Nettwerk Records, actually told *Glamour*: "We knew the media would come at us hard for that. And we tried, but I think you should question the artists who said no." Um, that is not it, Terry McBride. "No" is a complete sentence. Those artists who said no had their reasons and they do

10 Maerz, "The Oral History of Lilith Fair."

not owe him, or anyone, a reason for turning down Lilith Fair. Marty Diamond, Lilith Fair co-founder and booking agent, told *Vanity Fair* that it took "a lot of heavy lifting to get Erykah Badu [for the second year]. It took a lot of heavy lifting to get Missy Elliott. There were certainly artists like the Meshell Ndegeocellos of the world, that, by nature of who they were as artists, probably were a closer buy-in to participating." Like, first, there are no other Meshell Ndegeocellos. She is a singular talent and person. Diamond tells on himself in this quote but seems to think he's showing his commitment to diversifying Lilith Fair because of the "heavy lifting." Even Bonnie Raitt seems to still be making excuses, telling *Vanity Fair*, "You could make arguments like, 'Where's Latina and Native American and Asian acts?' But for the time, I thought that she couldn't have curated the shows any better than she did."

Ndegeocello told *Vanity Fair* that she was "very clear" what her role was when she joined Lilith Fair in 1998. (She also returned for 1999.) "But I don't have a problem with it — *get a real problem!* It was important to set the tour up so it would be successful, and that meant having acts that they knew would draw. I don't critique them for that. [But for me] sometimes it's hard to get an act to see where they fit in, or sometimes it's hard to create an environment where their music will be heard well. [At Lilith] you felt loved. And when you feel loved, you play well." Even in alluding to the challenges that Black artists might have faced when searching for personal and musical space at a festival where the headliners and crowds were dominated largely by white women, Ndegeocello has a lot of generosity towards Lilith Fair. This continued in a 2022 NPR feature celebrating the festival's twenty-fifth anniversary in which she credited Lilith Fair with helping her flourish as a musician. "Because I was out of the male gaze and music where it's just, you know, 'Show me what you got.' And it was more like, 'What can you make me feel?'"[11]

Lilith Fair's legacy holds multiple realities. It was a radical act and it was empowering, for both its artists and its audiences alike. It called out and threatened the patriarchal, sexist, and misogynistic barriers that had successfully excluded most women from full and equitable participation in the music industry. It didn't just bring "girls to the front"; it made them the entire goddamn show for three full summer festival seasons. But it also forecasted the limits of white feminism and a lack of representation at the top. Its vision of feminism lacked intersectionality, and its practice of feminism was deeply tied to commodification and late-stage capitalism. As a mainstream entity, it was as subversive as it could be. As a truly radical and progressive space? There was neither the will nor the market for it on a grand scale, so it had to come from the artists and acts themselves on an individual basis.

In some ways, Carlile has already resurrected Lilith Fair, just without the name and the baggage. But an annual weekend concert experience isn't the same scale as the sheer spectacle of Lilith Fair's ambitious and massive summer-long tour. I love that Carlile invokes Lilith Fair frequently and proudly states how it inspired her, a young queer woman looking for community and inspiration and representation in the

---

11 Lisa Weiner, "25 Years on, Lilith Fair Is a Reminder of How One Woman's Radical Idea Changed Music," *Morning Edition*, July 5, 2022, https://www.npr.org/2022/07/05/1108635464/25-years-on-lilith-fair-is-a-reminder-of-how-one-womans-radical-idea-changed-mus.

music industry. As Carlile half joked, she never left Lilith Fair and lives inside it every day, and I deeply appreciate her vision of Lilith Fair, which is overtly queerer and more inclusive of racialized artists. If anyone can do it, Carlile can, but I think a more expansive and radical Lilith is what we actually need. I'd love to see a Lilith Fair that prioritizes trans, gender diverse, Two Spirit, nonbinary, and queer artists, especially artists from historically excluded communities, as well as underrepresented genre artists. Hip hop, jazz, neo-soul, alt-R&B, metal, punk, and electronic artists would be exciting sonic additions to a reimagined Lilith Fair. Here's my starting pitch for a dream lineup: Carlile, Mitchell and McLachlan (of course), Alabama Shakes, Queen Latifah, Lido Pimienta, Christine and the Queens, Tracy Chapman, Ibeyi, Laura Jane Grace, Yola, Allison Russell, the Linda Lindas, Tanya Tagaq, Deborah Cox, Nelly Furtado, Big Freedia, Mitski, Emmylou Harris, Mickey Guyton, Shea Diamond, Gaelynn Lea, Vivek Shraya, the Yeah Yeah Yeahs, Sheer Mag, Yuna, Quanah Style, Ruby Waters, Tash Sultana, DijahSB, Rina Sawayama, and Rae Spoon.

Music can't solve everything, but it can be a place of inspiration, resistance, joy, and liberation. In the *Vanity Fair* oral history, writer Jessica Hopper (with Sasha Geffen and Jenn Pelly) called Lilith Fair "visionary," describing it as "glimpsing a possible future in which women were rightfully placed at music's center and not its margins." The center is as big a space as we want to make it; the scarcity model, the competition, the inequity and inequality — that's patriarchal, white supremacist, late-stage capitalism at work. Like Carlile, plenty of us have been living in Lilith Fair's vision since that first show in 1997. Hell, lots of people got there before Lilith Fair, for sure, but Lilith Fair's seismic disruption of the music industry was enough to cause a massive backlash that we've only begun to analyze and name over the last decade. As the thirtieth anniversary of Lilith Fair approaches, could McLachlan find the right co-conspirators — and the political will and social capital — to reinvest in a radical Lilith Fair revolution? I say yes, but first *she* has to want to.

ADVENTURES IN SEXISM

Media, Music Critics, and Mucking up the Boys' Club

It's hard to pinpoint the first time I realized I mattered less to somebody because I was a girl.

I was lucky. Many girls grow up in homes where they are taught from birth that they are secondary to and in service of fathers, brothers, uncles, and grandfathers. But I never really knew sexism in that way. I'm sure I internalized certain things — some everyday sexisms like girls were supposed to be dainty and boys were rough were somewhat normalized — but I was also the little girl with the curl in the middle of her forehead, so when I was good I was very, very good and when I was bad, I was horrid. There was an implicit understanding that I could never be a normal "good girl" because of my damn curl. It was my get-out-of-jail card from the age of three.

Since it was just my sister and me, there was no competition between me and a brother or another male. My male cousins were all at least five years younger than me. Basically, I ruled. All of the confidence that the adults felt about my abilities got poured into me while I was the only grandchild for the first thirteen months of my life. As I grew up, I was always helping my dad out in his business. I shopped for the Christmas presents. I was the equal of my father, the equal of anybody.

Except when I was eventually told I wasn't, and when it was heavily implied that me being a girl rendered me less worthy, capable, or important than someone who was a cisgender boy. I don't remember a distinct turning point, but at one time I felt free of gendered expectations, and then suddenly I was encumbered by them and by then I couldn't stop recognizing sexism even if I tried. I saw how things worked in certain classrooms or at other social functions beyond my circle of friends; I saw the ways in which some women had to tiptoe around their husbands' and boyfriends' volatile moods, how sons were prioritized above their sisters, the ways that some men talked only to other men or were only nice to women they found attractive.

It got worse, or at least more obvious, when I got older and was covering for my dad at his store or at the flea market and men would ask who was in charge or immediately try to talk me into a lower price because I was a girl. As some of my friends started pairing off and finding boyfriends, some of their parents would look at me with pity, and the pity felt layered. I was fat so what boy would like me, but also I was a girl and didn't I want to grow up and get married and have a family? The triple threat of anti-fatness, misogyny, and sexism is something I'll be unpacking and unlearning forever, but I remember the not-so-subtle hints that boys like certain kinds of girls. One relative even went so far as to say that he had even liked a fat girl when he was younger, but he was too afraid of ridicule to pursue it. This was said as a means of offering me an explanation as to why a boy I liked would make out with me in secret but never openly. I think my feminism grew three sizes that day. I knew in my gut that I deserved more than cowardice and shame. It took me a few more years to fully articulate it, but from that day on, I always believed I deserved to be loved for exactly who I am.

***

My feminism had its roots in my relationship with my father, and it had manifested wholly by 1993, fuelled entirely by the fact that, at fourteen years old, I knew sexism was an active choice made by willfully ignorant people. As much as my father and grandmother deserve lots of credit for instilling in me a belief in my own worth, it was an unlikely assortment of male teachers in my high school years and one woman student instructor who reaffirmed this idea on a daily basis. It was the norm for me to have strong men regard me as an equal, but for most of my girlfriends, this was an entirely different experience to their home lives. They had either part-time or absent fathers, or fathers so steeped in patriarchy that they thought of daughters as obligations or burdens or property, but never as worthy, independent persons. My English teacher, Mr. Fanning, and my music teacher, Mr. Smith, probably didn't even know they were strengthening my feminism, but because of their constant encouragement and the ways in which they treated every student equally, they became my unwitting feminist ambassadors. A woman student instructor, Anna Nobile, factored hugely into shaping me as a writer by encouraging me, affirming that my voice had merit and that it deserved to take up space. It was the after-school creative writing program that she put on at the University of British Columbia that pointed me towards the University of Victoria's creative writing program. She and

Mr. Fanning both helped me put together my portfolio in those shaky months following my father's death.

My earliest feminist foundations, though, came from the pop culture I consumed as a kid. There were many aspects of '80s pop culture that reinforced girls and women as passive participants in their own lives, but I held fast to my favourite strong, stubborn, flawed role models, and Miss Piggy was chief among them. I was always a fat kid. I'm still a fat kid. Miss Piggy was the be-all and end-all to me. She was a diva, yes, but she was also vulnerable, smart, funny, sarcastic, angry, confident, delightful, mean, and vivacious. To this day, I find myself understanding her better than almost any other fictional character in the world. She simultaneously breaks my heart and inspires me.

Complicated women were and are close to my heart. Fictional characters from *Golden Girls* continue to inform many of my decisions, as do Clair and Denise Huxtable, Murphy Brown, and Diane Chambers. I plucked Judy Blume books off the shelves and buried myself inside characters that were fucked up and fully realized. I devoured Christopher Pike's books. The weird feminist teenage thriller *Daughters of Eve* both incited and inspired me. The women in all of these books stood out in sharp contrast to the broken female narratives I also devoured like the Sweet Valley High series, which was packed with clichés and stereotypes, and anything by Lurlene McDaniel who wrote largely about girls who were dying, afflicted with disease, or coping with some life-altering diagnosis. Manipulative and narrow, they were small, fragmented pieces that never quite added up to real, living girls.

Within the archaic context of the gender binary, I think a lot about what it means to be a girl or a woman, and how that differs from what it means to be a boy or a man. Obviously that's a big, complicated, million-piece jigsaw of a puzzle, but let's break it down to something small, like a woman's success. How often does a woman's victory simply get to be her own celebration, her own achievement? It often becomes politicized or sexualized or gendered or racialized or economized or socialized rather than being simply a victory for the woman who achieved it.

Céline Dion's successes were presumed to be absent of her own agency, a pop diva in training from the instant René Angélil Svengalied her from the limited market of Quebec and transformed her into an international superstar. Dion was just a voice, while Angélil was a mastermind and businessman (and arguably something more predatory) who moulded a young girl with big dreams and a big voice into a pop sensation. That version of events isn't just disturbing, it's gross, and I've seen it and heard it perpetuated not just by male music critics but feminist pop culture scholars whose assumptions are no better than the misogynistic assholes they rail against. I've always been a proponent of the notion that people should look around and see who's agreeing with them, look at who is co-championing their cause and aligning with their thoughts. Because sometimes the very people you think you're fighting against are making the same point but in a different way — a dangerously different way. One of the most obvious examples of this are TERFs (trans exclusionary radical feminists), who claim to be feminists but are as anti-trans as far-right evangelical zealots fuelled by hate, fear, and misinformation.

It sucks, but part of my growing up meant coming to the terrible realization that women never get to just exist as people. And within women, there are still further ways to isolate, discriminate, and hate. The world is fucked up and the fight is always on. With men — and implicitly white cisgender straight men — as the basis of what constitutes a person, in every written, official, and documentable and meaningful way, women are constantly faced with an identity that is in contrast to, in opposition to, complementary to, and supplementary to, but never just human. It's easy to pretend we're just people, but there's overwhelming evidence to the contrary, even in something as relatively frivolous as the music industry.

As late as 1987, women were rarely ever a factor in periodicals like *Musician* magazine. When its editors celebrated a decade of "incredible" interviews with twenty-eight important artists, they included just two women and both were white: Joni Mitchell and Rickie Lee Jones. However, there must have been more women to include because the following year, the magazine changed tracks, putting Sinéad O'Connor on the cover and writing about "why the best new artists of 1988 are women" and how the major labels were changing their tune. Surely those women were making music only a year before.

A decade later, music magazines again "discovered" women. In 1997, a significant amount of ink was devoted to a "new" trend — have you heard? They're called women and girls and they make music. *Rolling Stone* released its "Women in Rock" issue and a companion book for its thirtieth anniversary, while *Spin* touted the "Girl" issue. At long last, the music industry was resplendent with women! Feminism for the win? Hold up a second. Even where women-centred lists were crafted as celebration rather than segregation, the underlying messaging was that music was a male space and women were merely the guest stars. As a music journalist I've been guilty of this myself, but I've never meant to position women as trends; rather I've tried to amplify their achievements. Sometimes, I've gone about this the right way. Is it a periodical expressly for and about women? If yes, then a women-centred list makes sense. But if it's *Rolling Stone* or *Spin*, the implication is women are Other. When there's an absence of gender parity within a publication's pages, the real way to celebrate women in music is to write more about women all the time, not once a year.

It's also important to hold the media accountable for how they write about women. There are small but critical differences in how questions differ between subjects: focusing solely on the emotional side of a woman's music and emphasizing sentiment over substance, asking a woman about her family and how she balances that family with her work, and applying narratives that are less about listening to her or her songs and more about the interviewer's idea of what constitutes a "lady interest."

Or, as is too often the case, when male writers focus more on a woman's body than on her art, such as James Hannaham's 1995 *Spin* cover story on Morissette that opens with "I shouldn't be here. From a vantage point not ten feet away, I'm watching Alanis Morissette grind her arms and legs through a vigorous workout on an obsolete stationary bicycle — the kind where the handlebars go back and forth. Minutes earlier, her tour manager had firmly instructed me to keep my distance." After Morissette's tour manager indicates the writer cannot go in, that they'll see him at dinner, Hannaham laments, "But how could he expect me to obey orders knowing that, over in the hotel exercise room, the pop banshee of the moment was sweating her booty off?"

He goes on to describe her in a variety of ways throughout the feature: "sweathog grunting," "video vixen," "flirtatious," a "hair twirler." Eventually Hannaham digs into the music and seems to treat her as an actual artist, until he drags her parents into it, inferring in his own way that they could be ashamed of her, writing, "She takes care to explain that her parents aren't fazed by hearing their daughter refer to oral sex and fucking to the cheers of an enthusiastic throng." What Morissette actually says, one assumes when prompted by Hannaham, is "A lot of people ask my parents, 'Aren't you embarrassed that your daughter speaks like that?' and they say, 'No, she's been that way her whole life, she just wasn't doing it publicly. And we're glad she is now.' . . . My mother's raunchier than I am."[1]

Between 1993 and 1997, arguably the build-up to what was ultimately considered peak "lady times" in terms of global success, Dion, Twain, Morissette, and McLachlan were alternately hyped and decimated in the press, and almost always with a gleeful fervour. Even when the media was ostensibly favourable, a detour into sexism seemed inevitable. Particularly because sexism can be so utterly casual, even from one's own allies:

> "She's not a fragile little girl. She's a very confident, intelligent, funny woman who knows what she wants and how to get it. And yet she remains so very nice." — Polly Anthony, the president of Dion's U.S. label, "praising" the star in *Billboard*, 1996[2]

---

1 Hannaham, "Alanis in Wonderland."

2 Chuck Taylor, "550's Celine Dion."

> "The girl doesn't seem to do anything wrong for us." — Ed Climie, director of buying for massive chain the Wall, "praising" McLachlan in *Billboard*, 1997[3]

> "It has a little bit of guts to it; it's not a wimpy record at all. Some songs make you cringe, like some of the Jewel stuff. On modern rock, it's good for about five minutes, then people start throwing stuff at the radio." — Paul Peterson, program director of modern rock, KZON Phoenix, on McLachlan's "Building a Mystery" in *Billboard*, 1997[4]

The non-allies were much more explicitly sexist, though Dion, Twain, Morissette, and McLachlan were all targeted in fairly specific ways.

Céline Dion

Dion was criticized for being dull, mechanical, and not sexy enough:

> "With her wrinkle-free alto and plain-Canadian-Jane image, Dion is arguably the most unthreatening diva ever to conquer the pop charts, and her bland-ambition appeal was sealed with the success

3 Larry LeBlanc, "McLachlan Comes to Fore on Arista Set," *Billboard*, June 28, 1997.

4 Chuck Taylor, "Sarah McLachlan's Recent Emergence on Radio Is Anything but a 'Mystery,'" *Billboard*, September 6, 1997.

> of last year's multiplatinum *Falling Into You.*" — David Browne, *Entertainment Weekly*, 1997[5]

> "With her attempt at soul, you can categorize Dion as fairly shallow, sort of a female Michael Bolton." — Brad Webber, *Chicago Tribune*, 1994[6]

> "The Canadian crooner dabbles in more soulful and sophisticated textures, and at times her dilettantism pays off. But she often falls back on her characteristic platform of polite, predictable schmaltz." — Elysa Gardner, *Los Angeles Times*, 1996[7]

"Unthreatening," "plain-Canadian-Jane," "fairly shallow," "dilettantism," and "polite, predictable schmaltz" are all so specifically sexist in their own small ways.

As Dion's fame grew, the story became less about her work ethic and talent and more about her marriage and starting a family. A 1997 profile in *People* revealed that Dion hated travelling without her husband/manager, that it was "weird, because I don't care about seeing the beauty of foreign countries if he's

---

5 David Browne, "Celine Dion and Michael Bolton: Yawn," *Entertainment Weekly*, November 21, 1997, https://ew.com/article/1997/11/21/celine-dion-and-michael-bolton-yawn/.

6 Brad Weber, "Celine Dion: The Colour of My Love," *Chicago Tribune*, February 17, 1994, https://www.chicagotribune.com/1994/02/17/celine-dionthe-colour-of-my-love-epic/.

7 Elysa Gardner, "Making a List? Checking It Twice? Here Are Some Guidelines to Keep Befuddled Spouses, Parents of Teenagers and Others on the Right Track," *L.A.Times*, December 8, 1996, https://www.latimes.com/archives/la-xpm-1996-12-08-ca-6855-story.html.

not there." Even now, almost decades later and happily married myself, this sentiment makes me angry. The article revealed oddly intimate details — a history of irregular periods, how much they enjoy sex, and Dion's desire to start a family and change diapers when not singing to the backs of the stadium. Superstar and devoted wife, right?

> "If it happens, it happens," says Dion of motherhood. "If it doesn't, it doesn't." In any case, she adds with a grin, "Rene and I are having a wonderful time trying."[8]

Gross. And there's no way in hell that a male musician's baby-making schedule would ever form any part of a profile on him. Not unless it was about all his illegitimate children because as a dude he just couldn't keep from spraying his seed like a busted fire hydrant in the middle of summer.

Shania Twain

Twain's success was never portrayed by media as her own. It was always a by-product of marrying well or looking swell:

> "[Shania Twain's] the highest paid lap-dancer in Nashville." — Steve Earle[9]

---

8 Karen S. Schneider and Jeanne Gordon, "Changing Her Tune," *People*, March 3, 1997.

9 Peter Blackstock, "Steve Earle — Can't Keep a Good Man Down," *No Depression*, April 1, 1996, https://www.nodepression.com/steve-earle-cant-keep-a-good-man-down/.

I love Steve Earle, but fuck you, Steve Earle.

> "While her sentiments are pretty naïve, her pipes sound plenty experienced" and Twain gives "enough passion to make us temporarily forget her pinup looks." — Bob Cannon, *Entertainment Weekly*, 1997[10]

This was written about Twain's song "God Bless the Child." Is that really the song on which you want to call her out as naive and "praise" Twain for singing well enough that you forgot you wanted to have sex with her? Good job, Twain. I'm sure she was pretty grateful to read that the writer managed to relieve himself from his hard-on long enough that he could write that review with his dick.

> "Shania's not singing. She's just, well, appearing. She's here to celebrate a marvel of marketing genius known as Fan Appreciation Day, a four-hour autograph-signing session, photo op and smile-athon . . . Her luscious brown hair is pulled back into a carefully styled ponytail, her cropped red turtleneck shows off a tantalizing swatch of midriff and her black stretch pants outline her curvaceous hips. Shania, 30, looks at the crowd and waves. She smiles a perfect, genuine smile. The crowd roars again. With a smile like that, who needs to sing? . . .

10 Bob Cannon, "God Bless the Child," *Entertainment Weekly*, January 31, 1997, https://ew.com/article/1997/01/31/god-bless-child-2/.

> She's the Mall of America's ideal of what a woman should be: kind, pretty, generous, unthreatening."
> — Karen Schoemer, *Newsweek*, 1996[11]

This is such a weird story, since it's choosing to cover an event where Twain is not singing but signing autographs, thus ensuring the writer will have nothing musical about which to actually write, only Twain's appearance, personality, and demeanour. Though that last sentence hints at a more subversive purpose by the author, the article never actually gets there.

> "It's not the typical country music success story: struggling Canadian singer works one-nighters across Canada for years, finally nets a U.S. record deal, chooses a rock producer (as a producer and husband), quits touring, and goes triple platinum with her second album." — Chet Flippo, *Billboard*, 1995[12]

Flippo framing Twain's success as mostly attributable to the acquisition of a rock producer and husband is such basic and obvious sexism that it would almost be boring if it weren't so infuriating.

---

11 Karen Shoemer, "Malling of Shania," *Newsweek*, February 26, 1996.

12 Chet Flippo, "Mercury Finds Longterm Success in Shania Twain," *Billboard*, December 9, 1995.

Alanis Morissette

Morissette was dismissed and disqualified by critics for being many things: young, a woman, angry, too sexual, not talented, having a pop past, and more:

> "How could a goofy-grinned, Rapunzel-haired former teen disco queen who once opened for Vanilla Ice beat out Elvis Presley and the Beatles? . . . At a time when teens and twentysomethings are going in for multiple piercings and tattoos just to feel something, is it any wonder Morissette's angry growl would catch on? And should we really be surprised, in this age of confessional TV talk, that there'd be a market for Alanis' no-details-spared view of sexuality — she did what in a movie theater? . . . [Morissette] has clearly nailed a cultural taproot, and the funny thing is, she's done it by incorporating elements of many of the women rockers who have come before her. She's got Carole King's hippie dress code down, Janis Joplin's tortured wailing, Mariah Carey's diva-next-doorishness, and Madonna's in-your-face sexuality. In fact, underneath it all, maybe Morissette is just an old-fashioned grrrl. Now, wouldn't that be ironic?" — David Hochman, *Entertainment Weekly*, 1996[13]

13 David Hochman, "Alanis Morissette," *Entertainment Weekly*, December 27, 1996, https://ew.com/article/1996/12/27/3-alanis-morissette/.

It's so very clever of Hochman to invoke Vanilla Ice and a bunch of Disney-related references in the opening sentence. He also obviously gets teen culture, all the tattoos and piercings and pain just to jolt us from our ennui. Plus, how dare Morissette believe she's her own person when clearly she's been Frankensteined together out of a collection of other gendered musician stereotypes who've had the nerve to masquerade as people all this time?

> "Alanis Morissette, the 22-year-old Ottawa native, is arguably, since the recent eclipse of *Baywatch* babe Pamela Anderson Lee, the most influential Canadian in the pop culture field. Her year-old album *Jagged Little Pill* has sold over nine million copies in the U.S., and is still ensconced near the top of the charts. Asked in a June 27 Copley News Service interview to explain the nature of her art, the leading edge of the 'angry young woman' movement explained, 'I think the only message I'm trying to convey is that it's good to convey. To me, communication is next to godliness. To connect with someone, to tell them how you're feeling — whether it's unapologetically vulnerable, or anger, or happiness or fear, you know, anything — just as long as you're communicating.' This Maria Callas of the 'riot grrrl' set may have her virtues, but concision is not one of them. Decades ago, novelist E. M. Forster expressed the same sentiment in just two words:

> 'Only connect.'" — Kevin Michael Grace, *Alberta Report*, 1996[14]

Good one, Grace. Sexist, elitist, and invoking a classic colonialist male author as a model by which Morissette should have the good sense to craft herself in his image? Harsh burn.

> "'Head Over Feet': Isn't it ironic that rock's biggest-selling female still tries to sell herself as an artist on the edge? To perpetuate that image, Morissette ostentatiously tosses a few rules to the wind in her latest clip. She refuses to deliver a polished lip-synch, instead subbing what looks like rehearsal footage. Her other big idea — to center the whole video on a close-up of her puss staring out at you — comes via Sinead O'Connor's blubbery 'Nothing Compares 2 U.' It's a rip-off, don't ya think?" — Jim Farber, *Entertainment Weekly*, 1996[15]

This reads less like a music video review and more like what would now be a Facebook rant, rife with sexist language and impotent rage.

> "We all have revenge fantasies, but few of us ride our peeved daydreams to the top of the charts. This year we delegated that task to Alanis Morissette,

14 Kevin Michael Grace, "Brevity, the Soul of Wit," *Alberta Report*, July 8, 1996.

15 Jim Farber, "Music Videos," *Entertainment Weekly*, November 1, 1996, https://ew.com/article/1996/11/01/music-videos-2/.

> a 21-year-old Canadian whose scorching single 'You Oughta Know' turned an otherwise banal experience — getting dumped — into the banshee howl of a jilted goddess. Revenge is sweet. Not only did the song hurl her *Jagged Little Pill* toward platinum sales — despite critical scorn (see 1995's worst albums) — it justified Madonna's Maverick Records and made it kinky to go to the theater." — Jeff Gordinier, *Entertainment Weekly*, 1995[16]

Seriously, *Entertainment Weekly*, do something else with your obviously misogynistic mid-'90s rage. Don't you know? Ladies are just trends! They'll be gone soon enough, according to your own calculations.

Sarah McLachlan

McLachlan, according to arts writers, ruined music with her lady parades, feminism, and youth.

> "You may think this summer's all-female, mostly folkie Lilith Fair tour opened commercial doors for women in rock; conversely, its small army of bleating confessionalists may have further stultified America's already moribund music scene." — *New York Magazine*, 1997[17]

16 Jeff Gordinier, "4 Grumpy Young Women," *Entertainment Weekly*, December 29, 1995.

17 Nightlife concert listings, *New York Magazine*, October 13, 1997.

This was just a listing for Lilith Fair. Not even an article, but a one-sentence blurb that manages to wedge in "bleating confessionalists" and "already moribund music scene" into the back half of its overly smug, self-congratulatory epithet.

> "McLachlan obviously places herself in the category of the self-defined, strong, female songwriter; her lyrics are mature with a capital M, to the point of sophomoric pseudo-profundity. She calls this record "a document of a world failing, of humanity failing," which, coming from a 26-year-old, is pretty fucking self-important. It's like using navel-contemplation as a lens for writing about the world. McLachlan's music is glossy and glib, with a dynamic range as flat as Cindy Crawford's stomach . . . *Fumbling* comes off like a *Reader's Digest* version of the artsy, mythology-obsessed female songwriter. This Romantic tradition has served women from Sandy Denny to Tori Amos well, but there are few real demons in McLachlan's songs. Good autobiographical music doesn't just tell the truth: it tells it with all the confusion and complexity left intact. *Fumbling Towards Ecstasy* is an easy-listening portrait of a woman — a perfectly graceful, confident, and smart woman — but it's not the portrait of an artist." — Joy Presse, *Spin*, 1994[18]

18 Joy Presse, "Sarah McLachlan: Fumbling Towards Ecstasy," *Spin*, March 1994.

Well, Jesus, this is depressingly sexist and it's written by a woman. If it were just a purely critical assessment, fine, but it's not. It's demeaning and ageist.

That prevailing ageism, particularly against Morissette and McLachlan, was as ridiculous then as it seems now. While age does sometimes bring nuance and emotional maturity, it doesn't invalidate the talent or feelings of a teenager or a young woman. The very reason *Jagged Little Pill* registered and resonated with so many people is that there are no feelings more true, raw, overwhelming, or passionate than the devastation of youthful ideals — romantic, emotional, intellectual, or otherwise. We've all been there. Let's stop pretending that's not when we felt most alive or most dead. Those moments don't get to be dismissed simply because they were felt and thought in our youth. Those are the moments at the foundation of everything we become, everything we reject, and everything that's ahead.

Devaluing youthful voices doesn't make one's grown-up voice better; it makes for a short-sighted, narrow definition of living, and it stinks of privilege. To ignore or silence youth is to render one's self obsolete. Youth matters, youth inspires, youth deserves more than just simple disdain or a pat on the head. And the youth of today and tomorrow would benefit if everyone would shut up and let the creative, smart, passionate people be heard, regardless of age.

In 1995, *Billboard*'s chief editor, the late Timothy White, was the first person to write about Morissette's *Jagged Little Pill*, weeks before the album's release. It's a wonderfully refreshing piece; he doesn't invalidate her feelings and experiences just because of her youth but rather takes them seriously, engages and considers them, and celebrates her as an artist. "Because she dares to stand naked in her remembrances, the narrator allows herself no comfort zone for self-righteousness, and as she builds steam in her incantatory checklist of public indignities and private indiscretions, the singer's wounded outrage mingles with a gathering courage that gives the listener a giddy desire to cheer her on," White writes.[19] He was one of the few critics who bolstered Morissette from the beginning. Many others repeatedly challenged her authenticity as an artist, failing to understand why this unproven twenty-one-year-old was fast becoming the best-selling musician in the world.

The mid-'90s were a particularly strange time. Alongside the increased visibility and dominance of women musicians, there was another cultural shift running parallel — one that was simultaneously celebrated as an emotional reckoning and dismissed as "victim culture," possibly the most insensitive and disgusting term ever invented to obfuscate blame and responsibility and perpetuate victim blaming and shaming.

In 1995, *Entertainment Weekly*'s David Browne wrote that "Morissette's seemingly overnight success is almost a textbook example of how to create a rock star."[20] Among his surefire steps to achieving a *Jagged Little Pill*–like blockbuster? Make a record that "feeds into today's popular victim culture." He cited a few examples of challenges Morissette had faced, including getting mugged

19 Timothy White, "Morissette's 'Jagged' Self-Healing," *Billboard*, May 13, 1995.

20 David Browne, "Working the 'Jagged' Edge," *Entertainment Weekly*, October 20, 1995, https://ew.com/article/1995/10/20/working-jagged-edge/.

in 1993 after moving to L.A. and seeking treatment for depression "brought on by loneliness." He also hypothesized that perhaps her depression was "brought on by the realization that being big in Canada doesn't necessarily translate south of the border," which doesn't even make sense since he was writing the article because of her "overnight" success and popularity, but okay. He concluded by stating "whatever the motivation, calculated or inadvertent, *Jagged Little Pill* is a mail-order catalog of grievances anyone, male or female, can relate to — call it talk-radio pop."

There's a callousness in the ease with which Browne chalks up a woman's experience to "victim culture." Disappointingly, that thread was prominent in Gerri Hirshey's epic *Rolling Stone* feature in 1997. In it, Hirshey interviewed some of the most important women musicians of the '90s and presented two distinct factions: women who deal *in* pain and women who deal *with* pain.

At one point, Hirshey lauds resiliency as being critical to surviving in the music industry, advising that if "you encounter a woman possessed of unusual tensile strength, it behooves you to settle in and listen up."

Provided, it seems, you're listening to the right woman.

Hirshey recounts a 1993 interview with Tina Turner, prior to the release of *What's Love Got to Do with It?*, the movie version of Turner's autobiography. Hirshey recalls the many abuses Turner suffered in her relationship with her husband, Ike:

> "Given that we are now living in the Age of Victimhood, a time when our commander in chief can talk about 'feeling your pain,' might this film cast Tina as a textbook victim of domestic violence?"

> "Victim?" she bellowed. "Victim! Gimme a break!"
>
> I'd baited her, I admitted — and was gratified by her outraged response. I'd been cranky as a wet cat about the '90s tsunami of public confessionals and celebrity spewings — couldn't take a second more of Sally Jesse purring, "I hear you."
>
> "Oh, I'm with you about that victim thing," Tina said. "It's everywhere. And I don't think it does anyone any good."
>
> Then Tina got on one of her Acid Queen rolls: "Someone tells me I was a victim, I become angry. I was not a victim . . . I was in control of everything I was doing."
>
> She didn't leave Ike earlier because she promised she'd stay till they made it big. She liked the man. And she had some far heavier responsibilities: "There was a mother there," she bellowed. "To Ike, to the children. Not this sniveling . . . little weak woman. They had me crying in the film script, and I said, 'I never cried that much in my life.'"

Hirshey goes on to praise Bonnie Raitt for being similarly stoic and for packing "two decades of womanly experience" — alcoholism, infidelity, record industry problems — into her Grammy Award–winning record, *Nick of Time*. Raitt, in Hirshey's estimation, "knows how to make enlightened complaining an exuberant art form rather than a whine." She continues by connecting Tori Amos and Alanis Morissette to her assessment of Raitt:

> Contrast Turner's and Raitt's steely reserve to the outpourings of Tori Amos, a woman of the next generation. Amos is part of the singer-songwriter vanguard now turning pain into platinum. She went public with her trauma as a rape victim in "Me and a Gun," a cut from her *Little Earthquakes* album. It was, she said, a true and powerful statement. But she had this to say about the Gen X compulsion for hand-wringing: "I think our generation loves our pain, and if you dare fucking take it away from us, we'll kill you. We like our pain. And we're packaging and selling it."
>
> Amos' wry assessment might help explain the roaring success of Morissette's collection of danceable diatribes — most notably "You Oughta Know," the poison valentine to an ex-lover that was a huge hit in 1995. Given Morissette's first rock outing in 1990 as mall-rat-with-mike and a serious hair-volumizer habit, it's understandable that many critics viewed her brand-new angsty-me with a certain amount of cynicism. But her mass appeal seemed undeniable. *Jagged Little Pill* sold more than 11 million copies and won two Grammys — ample testament to the current lively market for the well-amped kvetch.[21]

In addition to the remarkable insensitivity of comparing Amos's song about her rape to whining rather than "exuberant art,"

21 Hirshey, "The Nineties."

there's something incredibly ugly at work in this piece. There's a harshness that breaks my heart, since it feels so much like it's written from the perspective of a person who has been told her own traumas don't deserve or merit consideration. I respect that survival comes in many forms, but it needn't come at the expense of compassion. And yet so much music journalism, at least from certain publications, is written with a barbed-wire approach, as if cruelty and cool detachment are the same as critical engagement.

In an article titled "Quiet Grrrls," *Newsweek*'s Karen Schoemer writes, "Call us insensitive, but when we first heard about Lilith Fair we had one reaction: run." She goes through a laundry list of rote descriptors — "touchy-feely," "girl-friendly," "artsy-craftsy" — before breaking out the really loaded adjectives for the performers: "pious heavyweights," "fragile young flowers," etc. At one point Schoemer surmises, "This isn't entertainment — it's therapy."[22]

Coming of age between waves in the post-post-feminist landscape of the mid-'90s, my friends and I were all Angela Chases in a world full of Murphy Browns, and those two examples of feminist role models felt good. We hadn't yet chosen or prioritized ourselves; and though we didn't know how at the time, it felt like we could learn, and women like Morissette and McLachlan could help. They, too, had been caught up in the twisty wreckages of love and sex and crushing pressures, and they had survived to sing about it and write about it. They just had to dwell in the pain for a little while to release it.

---

22 Karen Schoemer with Yahlin Chang and Kate Cambor, "Quiet Grrrls," *Newsweek*, June 30, 1997.

But "victim culture" was just one form of attack. Women were also pitted against each other, praised in one sentence and undermined in the next. *Rolling Stone*'s Lorraine Ali joined the Lilith Fair tour for five days in the summer of 1997. Her account of that time likens the atmosphere to a high school society:

> A pecking order quickly forms: Suzanne Vega is the cool and distant art chick, Paula Cole the down-to-earth best friend, Jewel the stuck-up one, Tracy Chapman the respected activist and McLachlan the peppy student-body president who wears weird-colored eye shadow. The second-stagers — Mudgirl, Leah Andreone and Cassandra Wilson — are like the stoners in the smoking area, possessing the coolest clothes, attitudes and tattooed backup dudes. The Borders Stage's solo artists — Kinnie Starr and Lauren Hoffman — are the tag-along little sisters, still gawky, unpolished and apart from the social hierarchy.[23]

Ali's observations are good, if pointed, and infer a *Heathers*-like fracas bubbling under the surface of all the sisterly solidarity. At one point, Jewel tells Ali, "What's cool is, no one here acts like a star. It doesn't matter how many records you sell, even though I've sold the most." At a pre-show press conference, Sarah McLachlan recounts the industry-related sexism she faced when her record was pitted against Tori Amos's. Ali muses that "maybe the fact that there's little air time allotted to women

23 Lorraine Ali, "Backstage at Lilith," *Rolling Stone*, September 4, 1997.

explains the underlying sense of competitiveness at these press events, which resemble the uncomfortable alliance of a NATO meeting. Answers are filled with feminist-sounding words like empowerment, community and even germination, and the participants look as detached from one another as a seated row of subway riders."

Ali wraps up the piece in L.A., where "the veneer begins cracking." Cassandra Wilson is upset about not being asked to play the main stage, and another artist has accused McLachlan of "stealing her quotes to use in press conferences." It's a damning bit of tour reportage, and it's well crafted, but it feels sexist. It certainly paints a very specific picture that feeds into the stereotype that women simply can't get along.

The flipside is that while Morissette and McLachlan were somewhat embraced and/or scorned by mainstream music magazines for their post-feminist, modern attitudes, Céline Dion and Shania Twain were rejected because they weren't seen as cool enough. Karen Schoemer, who wrote about Twain's Mall of America appearance, comes out swinging at *Rolling Stone* and *Spin* for excluding Dion and Twain, asking, "What does it take to be a 'Woman in Rock?'" Schoemer's analysis is astute at times, but she, too, veers into women-bashing to convey her points. She argues that "Women in Rock" is no longer gender-specific but political, and that one must be "correctly" female. She tosses out phrases like "Fiona Apple-style fetishistic victimhood," and then opines that Twain and Dion do "womanhood the old-fashioned, unironic, hyperfeminine way." This is, she qualifies, because they "comb their hair and flaunt their bellybuttons, and it's not a statement. Their music is unabashedly domestic, without complicated subtexts." Schoemer asserts that it's "W.I.R. [Women in

Rock] suicide to say so, but in 1997 there's something weirdly refreshing about Dion and Twain's implacable refusal to ride the Girl Power bandwagon, and their unexpected outsider status. It actually takes some guts to be so unapologetically uncool."[24]

Schoemer ends her essay on a sort of progressive note, advocating for "Just Plain People in Rock," rather than continued gender segregation. If only she'd proven capable of writing an essay celebrating two women without insulting and ripping apart a million others, that would have strengthened her credibility substantially.

Even with the album sales and media buzz, researcher Allan Wells wasn't convinced that women artists dominating the conversation was tantamount to dominating the charts. At least not all of them. Upon a closer examination of the charts, he determined that hype didn't necessarily translate into sales or equitable radio presence for women in the '90s, and he wrote three different papers pertaining to the subject of women and music, ultimately reinforcing the notion that this was a trend rather than a substantial shift in the industry.

Another group of researchers felt Wells's assessment failed to consider numerous outside sources. This is an excerpt from "Gender and the Billboard Top 40 Charts between 1997 and 2007," a study published in *Popular Music and Society* in 2011, written by Marc Lafrance, Lara Worcester, and Lori Burns. In it, they cite Wells and his series of pieces examining the annual

24 Karen Schoemer, *Newsweek*, November 17, 1997.

Billboard Top 40 charts and women, including "Women in Popular Music," "Women on the Pop Charts," and "Nationality":

> Wells examines whether the apparent "rise of women artists" in the 1990s is confirmed by *Billboard* chart trends for the same period. Overall, he finds that "typically, men have double or more than women's scores. Even in women's best years, 1996 to 1999, the men's totals were considerably higher, and the number of hits was about double the women's. So much for female domination of music. The 1997–99 female performance is only marginally better than the late 1980s." (*Nationality* 226) Not surprisingly, these findings lead Wells to argue that, "despite some recent gains, it is obvious that female success in popular music is well below the media hype." (*Nationality* 229) Similarly, Wells argues that while the charts indicate "the presence of legitimate female stars" they also indicate that "female success is not very deep; indeed it may be as precarious as the next big hit." (*Nationality* 229) He concludes by arguing that "there is a very long way to go before women reach equality with men on the charts." (*Nationality* 229)

Now, there are a few things lacking in Wells's conclusions, particularly the snidely written "so much for female domination of music" and that "female success is not very deep; indeed it may be as precarious as the next big hit." Well, when women are thrust into the spotlight but are still silenced, excluded, and erased from the conversation as legitimate musicians, chances are the successes will not be as simple as examining a chart that measures an infrastructure set up to fuel men, the very men who can get radio play back to back, who are expected to dominate the music industry's largest factions. Following this logic, men are meant to co-exist on a playlist or a top 40 chart. They don't simply cancel each other out. Something very different happens when two women played back to back is considered too much chick band, too un–rock 'n' roll, too much like the beginning of a slumber party.

Wells's objection to the notion that women dominated music in the '90s was rooted on a very narrow window of data. Yes, men outperformed women on the charts in 1997 and 1998. But, as Lafrance, Worcester, and Burns wrote, a poorer showing on Billboard Top 40 charts doesn't negate the very real strides women were making in the music industry:

> While female artists then had two of their best chart performances in the years 1999 and 2000, these performances were relatively weak when considered alongside the "buzz" surrounding women in the world of popular music at the time. Yet, unlike Wells, we are not of the view that the relatively weak chart performances of female artists in the late 1990s could or indeed should be taken as proof that "women's success in popular music at the end of the 1990s was well below the media hype." (*Nationality* 229) We argue that this hype was entirely warranted; to understand it, however, it is necessary to go beyond the charts and consider

> social phenomena such as the rise of the Riot Grrrl movement (see Rosenberg and Garofalo), the popularity of the Lilith Fair concert tour (see Westmoreland), and the mainstream success of third wave feminism (see Rasmusson). When we consider phenomena such as these, we see that there are a number of good reasons why — at the dawn of the post-millennium — musicologist Susan McLary declared, "Women in the field of music today feel unusually optimistic, more so than at any previous time in Western history" (1245). Ultimately, then, we do not feel that women's success in the world of popular music at the end of the late 1990s can be reduced to their performance on the *Billboard* charts.[25]

And it's true. Women's success can't simply be measured in their chart performance. The Billboard charts measure a system that does not expect women to succeed. If anything, the music industry, and most of the related industries, actively worked against a woman's success — until, of course, they could monetize it.

25 Marc Lafrance, Lara Worcester, and Lori Burns, "Gender and the Billboard Top 40 Charts between 1997 and 2007," *Popular Music and Society* 34, no. 5 (2011): 557–570, https://doi.org/10.1080/03007766.2010.522827.

CANADA, MEN, MONEY, AND BUSTING "CHICK" MYTHS

Neil Young, Joni Mitchell, and Leonard Cohen brought Canada a certain notoriety in the U.S. in the '60s, and certainly the CanRock revolution took its shape in the '80s with Bryan Adams at the lead, but it wasn't until the '90s that the Canadian invasion became a truly global phenomenon.

The mid to early '80s were dripping with dudes. Women, on the other hand, were sparsely represented in Canadian music. It was basically *The Smurfs* — eighty men for every one woman — and it was dire. Proof of Canada's cock-rock paradise can be found well-documented in the hefty and thorough *Have Not Been the Same: The CanRock Renaissance, 1985–1995* by Michael Barclay, Ian A.D. Jack, and Jason Schneider. It's a great book, but damn, it's so heavy with dudes. But it's not necessarily the writers' faults; it's merely evident of the time period. They cover Julie Doiron, Rebecca West, Wild Strawberries, Jale, cub, and Sarah McLachlan, but even then, women are underrepresented in the tome's hundreds of pages.

When women are mentioned, some of the ways in which the stories get told are less than ideal. For example, a large portion of the considerable ink dedicated to McLachlan is actually occupied by the messy lawsuit between her and Darryl Neudorf, her co-writer and guitarist, who sued her and Nettwerk Records for royalties after she became hugely rich. Neudorf tells his side of the story in lengthy interviews, and while I'm sure the authors requested interviews with McLachlan, she does not go on record for whatever reason, so it's a very incomplete presentation of the "facts." It's a compelling story — it's juicy, gossipy, and it paints McLachlan in a vastly different light than the usual hippie, sensitive girl persona attributed to her. Instead she's portrayed as selfish, not actually writing songs on her own, hogging all the credit — it heavily favours Neudorf's version of events.

Canadian women musicians deserve more than that, and ultimately, they get it, not in that book but in media coverage and album sales. I don't know that there's any one formula that can be used to calculate why Dion, Twain, Morissette, and McLachlan were as huge as they were or what that says about Canada. Some informed guesses: the success of the CanRock revolution brought a lot of eyes and money to Canada; the CanCon rules created a demand that subsequently resulted in an investment in making Canadian music; women artists were standing out in sharp relief against the overly male market; women were becoming significant consumers in their own right and purchasing more music; and when one woman started to sell well, every other label wanted to present their own woman artist.

It's important to remember that Dion, Twain, Morissette, and McLachlan aren't anomalies, even if their success at the time was. The '90s may have ended with the feminist triumph that was Lilith Fair, but the entire decade had been a slow build to that particular groundswell. Beginning in tiny corners of Halifax,

Montreal, Toronto, and Vancouver and taking root in the burgeoning indie, underground, punk, and folk scenes, women jockeyed for prominence and credibility, sometimes supported by their male peers and allies, and other times excluded from the very real, penis-password-protected cisgender boys' club.

A host of other artists, from solo singer-songwriters to avant-punk bands, were dominating the underground, thriving and striving alongside or struggling at the edge of the spotlight. Not only were they making great music, thereby making Canada a more culturally dynamic and creative place, but the visibility of women taking up space in the music industry was critically important: it expanded and normalized society's version of what constitutes a band or a singer or an artist.

Twain and Morissette signed record deals with American labels, while Dion and McLachlan were signed by Canadian ones. Still, by 1997 all four were household names on both sides of the border, and their reach was growing around the world. Each occupied their own distinct space in pop culture, too, so all could flourish without that common sexist trope of suppressing one in favour of the other. Morissette's alt-rock came closest to McLachlan's pop-rock, but they were never positioned in competition with each other the way that McLachlan was forced to face off against American Tori Amos for radio play. Dion owned the adult contemporary arena, and Twain, country and country-pop.

Coming of age during this time period had a strange effect on me. As I was becoming more aware of the fact that I was a girl, and what it meant to be a girl, I was also witnessing the iconic rise of these four Canadian musicians. According to everything that Dion, Twain, Morissette, and McLachlan reflected back at me, I was powerful, I could be famous, my voice mattered, and I could rule the world. It didn't matter that I didn't look like them or that I didn't sing; I saw them valued as women, and I identified emotionally and intellectually with Morissette and McLachlan. Being a teenaged girl and finding role models who aren't just aspirational figures but who actually seem to get you, who unravel your Christmas lights tangle of feelings in their own songs, who make you feel seen and a little less alone is like the earth cracking open and a tiny flower pushing through, unfolding, free to grow even in a place it doesn't seem to belong.

There's no exact map that illustrates how Dion, Twain, Morissette, and McLachlan became Canada's best-selling Canadian artists, emerging as superstars where there had never been successful women of that magnitude before. But plenty of articles attempt to capture the zeitgeist of the Canadian invasion of the '90s.

In a 1997 *Maclean's* article, Canadian Academy of Recording Arts and Sciences president Lee Silversides gives credit to the Canadian content regulations that were introduced in 1971, stating, "It's taken that much time to finesse our ability to market it, at home and on the international stage."[1] The CanCon rules mandated that broadcasters must dedicate thirty percent of their airtime to Canadian artists. (It's now forty percent.) The system wasn't and isn't perfect, but it provided access to airplay for fledgling Canadian bands. More money went into

1 Diane Turbide, "Canada's Hit Parade," *Maclean's*, March 24, 1997.

developing Canadian talent, fan bases grew in support of homegrown acts, and a much more complex and prosperous industry evolved. In the '70s and '80s, Canadian acts definitely flourished at home and abroad, but the all-important factor was becoming a hit in the U.S. Anne Murray did it, so did Bryan Adams, but it wasn't until the late '80s and early '90s that two separate Canadian music scenes began to develop: mainstream — like Corey Hart, Glass Tiger, Maestro Fresh Wes, to name a few — and indie.

The grunge and alt-punk/pop happening in Halifax was just one aspect of Canada's flourishing independent music scene. Loreena McKennitt produced her own music under her own label and was so successful that the majors came calling. She opted to keep control of her music but made a lucrative distribution deal. Meanwhile, in Toronto, Barenaked Ladies were just a bunch of guys peddling their own tapes when a bidding war between major labels erupted, marking a turning point in indie Canadian acts levelling up to become mainstream.

According to a 1994 *Billboard* article, Canadian artists and songwriters had brought an excess of $250 million annually into the country in music-related revenue since 1990.[2] Dion and McLachlan were among those credited for the boom, but as of 1994, women weren't fully dominating the conversation. Yet.

It was a different story in 1995, when *Billboard* declared it was "celebrating the year of women," specifically Dion, Twain, and Morissette, whose records sold millions. The buzz was building, and according to a 1997 *Flare* article, fifteen thousand musicians sent demos to Canada's top six record companies

---

2 Larry LeBlanc, "Oh Canada! One Nation under a Groove," *Billboard*, February 5, 1994.

in 1996.[3] About a dozen signed contracts. By 1996, Morissette had broken debut album sales records (her earlier albums were released under the mononym Alanis, so *Jagged Little Pill* is often considered her debut under her full name) in both the U.S. and Canada, and by 1997, Dion's, Twain's, and Morissette's most recent records had sold 57 million copies worldwide. No wonder the Juno Awards created a brand new category for international achievement simply to honour those three women. McLachlan's own star had also been steadily rising: *Fumbling Towards Ecstasy* went double platinum; Lilith Fair revitalized the summer music tour scene; and *Surfacing* was about to make her a major player on American charts.

There are those who argue that mediocrity is no impediment to success. That's true. But there's also no reliable method with which to distinguish good music from bad. It's a matter of taste. It's easy to argue the things that might add up to "bad" music, such as too much Auto-Tune, overproduction, misogynistic lyrics, a lazy backbeat, too much cowbell, or not enough cowbell. Ultimately, bad and good don't mean much to most music fans, who listen not with a musicologist's ear or even a critic's ear but with their minds and hearts. In the same way that we don't all love the same person or the same cheese, we can't possibly all love the same music.

On the surface, though, it did seem that if you were a woman making music in 1997, it was your moment. In an interview with *Time* that year, Atlantic Records co-chairman Val Azzoli admitted that the industry embracing women was purely a business response to a previously untapped market. "Honestly, we in the

---

3 Liza Finlay, "Women Who Rock," *Flare*, April 1997.

record business are not leaders," she said. "We are a bunch of sheep. When one kind of record does well, we all follow with more like it."[4]

And often they came to Canada looking to strike gold again and again. *Billboard*'s Larry LeBlanc told *Maclean's* about the feverish fallout that resulted in him writing a tiny story about then twenty-one-year-old Oh Susanna. He'd "fallen in love with her voice," likening her to a combination of Hank Williams and Emmylou Harris, and wrote as much. Madness ensued. "The next thing I know, I'm fielding calls from Elliot Roberts, who manages Neil Young, and from Joe Boyd in London, who records the McGarrigle sisters, they wanted to know more about Oh Susanna. Then this woman, who hadn't even made a record — she'd sold a total of fifty self-produced cassettes — got called directly by DreamWorks, Steven Spielberg's company. That's how much the world's music industry is paying attention to Canadian talent."[5]

And the reason they were paying attention was largely thanks to Dion, Twain, Morissette, and McLachlan. Canada wasn't simply a land of talented people — our export was superstars. Global power players. The country's most successful musicians. Women.

Lilith Fair ended in 1999, and it felt like a definitive door had closed on a decade and that a certain movement had shifted,

4 Christopher John Farley, "Galapalooza! Lilith Fair," *Time*, July 21, 1997, https://content.time.com/time/subscriber/article/0,33009,986728-1,00.html.

5 Turbide, "Canada's Hit Parade."

both in Canada and around the world. The record industry, of course, was upended by the internet while indie music scenes flourished in Montreal, Toronto, Vancouver, Omaha, Seattle, Portland, North Carolina, Atlanta, Brooklyn, and L.A. Plus, a bold new generation of women were storming the charts in Canada and the U.S.

Morissette moved into different musical territory and only some of her fans followed, while Twain was gearing up for what would be her fourth record before taking almost two decades off from releasing new music. McLachlan and Dion continued to release albums and tour, with Dion — and subsequently, Twain — eventually taking up residence in Las Vegas and ushering in a whole new lucrative economic reality for superstar musicians with big back catalogues looking to perform for their fans but get off the road and into a more stable routine.

The 2000s proved that women weren't a musical trend but rather a substantial and robust part of the record business. What was clear, particularly as music moved into the latter half of the decade and the early part of the 2010s, was the relative absence of political messaging. There was no explicit feminism and no girl power, no fire or solidarity. For some people, "feminist" became a dirty word following Lilith Fair. Even McLachlan took to calling herself a humanist. And stars like Katy Perry, Taylor Swift, and Lady Gaga shied away from it so much that it became a major moment in the culture when in 2014, Beyoncé visibly aligned herself with the movement at the MTV Music Video Awards, pausing in the middle of her fifteen-minute medley performance in front of a giant screen that read "FEMINIST."

***

The fight to move beyond a moment is understandable. We fight, we hope to have achieved something, touch the sky, and settle back down. We grow and move on and leave a few things behind, like snakes shedding skin, like words falling beneath a red pen. Because we all learn differently and have varying capacities for understanding and empathy, we move at different speeds in our comprehension and internalization of nebulous concepts. Not everyone today understands that feminism needs to be intersectional, inclusive, and equitable, even though, as Audre Lorde said, "I am not free while any woman is unfree." Those of us who are part of historically repressed and excluded groups know that our rights are entwined because we've seen very clearly whose bodies count and whose bodies don't. Whose bodies are legislated and whose bodies are free.

As feminism has re-entered the public dialogue in a big way — primarily because of this intersectionality discussion and the rollback of reproductive rights in parts of the United States — it's proven to also be needlessly divisive in music. In some ways, it feels like the '90s all over again. It's thirty years later, and "feminism" is on the verge of becoming a dirty word, and some right-wing, libertarian, and contrarian types are doing their best to make "woke" an insult like they did with "politically correct." This time they're painting "cancel culture" as knee-jerk, reactionary, and hysterical instead of what it actually is: accountability. Feminism is supposed to be about dismantling the patriarchy. I've been told that over and over. Those who believe that the usefulness of feminism has expired might ask,

How did Dion and Twain do that? How could McLachlan's coffee shop confessionals and Morissette's mega-rage be feminist? How does any of it add up to women being empowered?

Those are all fair questions, but the fact remains that all of these artists empowered *me*. The '90s are critically important: I went from being an eleven-year-old who hadn't figured out bras to a twenty-one-year-old roughly navigating how to self-publish an alt-women's magazine, with all the crushing formative lows and rarified highs that youth, hormones, and rebellion bring.

I've been thinking back about how the cultural shift away from the '90s manifested itself musically. Over the last fifteen years, criticism and critical thinking has become (wrongly) synonymous with bullying and aggression, with truly critical reviews of music and other art forms dwindling in favour of social media posts that are written to maximize clicks with "hot takes." For over a decade, feminism — and the sort of thoughtful discussion on the roles of women in media that Shirley Manson liked to engage in during the '90s — sort of lurked in the shadows of pop culture and especially popular music. In 2013, *Huffington Post* even published a list of "10 Celebrities Who Say They Are Not Feminists,"[6] and it included quotes from the likes of Kelly Clarkson, Taylor Swift, Lady Gaga, and Björk. But feminism was a torch inside me and many of my friends, a soft glow in our centres that kept burning even when it wasn't at the forefront of popular conversation, even as more and more women seemed to move away from its confines, seeing it as a trap rather than a platform.

---

6 "10 Celebrities Who Say They Aren't Feminists," *Huffington Post*, December 17, 2013, https://www.huffpost.com/entry/feminist-celebrities_n_4460416.

In 2010, McLachlan attempted to resurrect Lilith Fair, but it proved a disastrous failure with multiple cancelled dates and sparse attendance. Fingers were pointed in multiple directions: poor organization, bad bookings, that society and women no longer needed a women's music festival. We were post-gender bias, just like we were supposedly post-racial. If you believe this, your privilege is showing. Go on and check yourself.

Oddly, 2023 is sort of a magical time to be a feminist. There's a new momentum, a fourth wave of women proudly identifying as feminists, refusing to buy into the associated stigma that has proliferated in their lifetimes, which is to say the last decade or so. But there is also an ongoing battle about what it means to be a feminist, and setting out a bunch of check marks won't solve this particular riddle. One of the modern interpretations is that women have to stick together — otherwise you're one of those mean girls, a real Heather, right? Probably not. Unwavering, obedient support is the MO of cult leaders and totalitarian regimes and doesn't favour racialized women or trans women, who rightly push back at the loud white majority in many feminist groups. Feminism stemmed from critical dialogues and evaluations of injustice, outrage, and demands for equality and representation. Feminism isn't silence, nor is it unanimous agreement — it's about equity, asking difficult questions that challenge the status quo, and dismantling systemic barriers.

In the summer of 2014, women musicians and women-fronted bands accounted for, on average, less than thirty percent of the lineups at Canada's music festivals. For example, Montreal's famed Osheaga music festival featured forty-nine all-male bands and just two all-women bands. Most major festivals continue to have significant gender bias in their headliners; a seventy/thirty split, at best, in favour of men is typical. In 2018, forty-five music festivals around the world, including four in Canada, pledged to achieve fifty/fifty gender parity in their artist lineups by 2022. Now, obviously this concept of fifty/fifty speaks to a gender binary that is well and truly old school at this point, but it was 2018's attempt at equality. Have any of those festivals lived up to that pledge? Unfortunately the Covid-19 pandemic, subsequent recession, and the climate emergency (catastrophic wildfires and air quality at festival locations) have upended live music, so there is no definitive answer.

The dismal percentages around programming women were never, as some tried to say, because there weren't enough women making music. It circles back to a question of visibility, bias, sexism, and willful ignorance. Women are making music, there's no doubt about that, particularly in Canada, and they represent brilliantly diverse genres. In 2014, a new generation of stars was emerging, with artists either finally getting the recognition they've long deserved or arriving fresh on the scene. Tanya Tagaq combined throat singing, metal, and electronica for a fascinating, visceral, and spine-tingling thrill. Toronto's Alvvays were the new indie scene saviours riding high on their surf-pop debut. There was also the garage-punk chaos of Vancouver's the Pack a.d. and Sackville, New Brunswick's Partner.

These days, I want to highlight more racialized, gender diverse, gender queer, agender, and nonbinary artists as well. Vivek Shraya is an incredible singer-songwriter (and author) who has poured herself into her magnetic pop music for two decades but who is only in the last few years finally receiving the recognition she deserves. Myst Milano's propulsive music (they're a composer, rapper, DJ, and activist) pulls from '90s house and hardcore to punk and ballroom. Their motto is "no genre, no gender, no rules." Pantayo is a quintet of queer artists from the Filipinx diaspora that fuses electronic music, synth-pop, R&B, and punk with kulintang. Debby Friday makes intricately layered electronic music that traverses every dance floor, whether you're rave-ready or enjoying a chill apartment hang. Singer-songwriter and folk musician Allison Russell just recently broke through as a solo artist after more than twenty years as a working musician. DijahSB is a rapper who is at turns heartfelt, hilarious, and endlessly inventive. Ruby Waters is a singer-songwriter who shifts and blends soul, pop, lo-fi, acoustic, and electronic influences. Mariel Buckley's country-folk story songs are densely packed with wry one-liners and devastatingly intimate observations. Elisapie has just released a gorgeous collection of covers of popular songs that she's lovingly translated from English into Inuktitut.

All of these artists are filling up and expanding the space that Dion, Morissette, Twain, and McLachlan created with their success. It's been almost thirty years and we've never come close to replicating the curious majesty of their domination, but we're still marvelling at the pieces of the glass ceilings they shattered. There wasn't a formula for their success; each established her own niche with very little overlap stylistically or musically. Even if one can parse complementary patterns in the marketing or the business plans, there's no single strategy that worked for all four.

I actually love that. I love that it's inexplicable. So many people attempt to quantify and qualify it: oh, it was the '90s, Lilith Fair, the Riot Grrrls were growing up; it was the year of women, girl power, etc. It's all of those things but also none of those things, too. Dion, Twain, Morissette, and McLachlan were part of the cause, not the effect. They worked hard, they hustled, they found people that championed them and their vision. They made music they were passionate about, that had a point of view and authenticity. Even Dion's saccharine romance-novellas-masquerading-as-songs — which likely felt like artifice to her naysayers — are rooted deeply in her hummingbird of a heart.

It's strange to analyze four women, dig inside their music, and sift through the public details of their lives. I'm glad I did, though, because it forced me to reckon with so many things, namely how I was trying to challenge sexism and misogyny without identifying my complicity and without seeing the bigger picture. I acted as a feminist gatekeeper while indulging in snobbery and devaluing a woman's worth by virtue of my relationship to her music.

My whole youth spun in, out, and around the ubiquity of Dion, Morissette, Twain, and McLachlan. Anybody who is part of historically excluded groups knows the warm glow of pride that manifests when someone "like you" succeeds. I took comfort in Dion's and Twain's success on the most basic level, like seeing another woman on the street and thinking, "Hey! They're a bit like me!" It was cursory acknowledgement and a tallying of potential allies. But I revelled in Morissette's and McLachlan's success, taking validation from it somehow as a fellow young woman of complicated emotional architecture who refused to shut up and sit pretty.

It's so easy to allow ironic detachment, disdain, mockery, and other dilutants to create emotional absences and displace us from our foundations. It's easy to brush off something as a mainstream fluke, or to take the success of Dion, Morissette, Twain, and McLachlan as evidence of Canada's ability to monetize, leverage, and infect the world with its unthreatening mediocrity. But that narrative erases the victories and obscures the triumphs of these artists; it diminishes their importance and devalues their contributions.

Dion's, Morissette's, Twain's, and McLachlan's legacies are reminders to reconcile my opinions with my values every day; to write responsibly and respectfully about music, think critically about my complicity, and champion artists who work hard and who resonate with people other than me; to challenge all the stupid ways we derail and deride women with everyday sexism and deliberate misogyny. Millions of people consumed and consume their music. Record sales were through the roof, obviously. But there were almost as many people doing everything in their power to discredit and demolish their success.

Well, suck it, haters. These four women are still among the most successful Canadian artists in Canada, and in all likelihood, thanks to changes in the record industry and lagging sales, they will remain at the top. They are symbols, yes, but also, for me, touchstones of my youth. The soundtrack to my teenaged feminism. Pockets to tuck myself inside to safely grieve, or wreak some havoc, or just lose myself in who I used to be.

In 2015, this was, according to Nielsen SoundScan, the list of the best-selling artists in Canada. Ever.

1. Céline Dion
2. Alanis Morissette
3. Shania Twain
4. Whitney Houston
5. U2
6. Sarah McLachlan
7. Eminem
8. The Beatles

9. Andrea Bocelli
10. Diana Krall

It's a snapshot of a time but it's also a turning point in Canada, around the world, and in my own tiny universe. Dion, Morissette, Twain, and McLachlan. Bigger than the Beatles. That sounds about right.

THE '90S REVIVAL, NOSTALGIA, AND JUSTICE FOR "PROBLEMATIC" WOMEN

When I published the first iteration of this book in 2015, I saw these beautiful Doc Martens at the Bay, a Canadian department store. They were black leather but not super shiny, and they had higher tops than the Docs I had as a teen in 1993. But the thing that made me stop immediately and begin to covet them was the floral motif, both on the satin ribbon laces and on the inside of the boot, so when you folded down the higher tops, the floral satin revealed itself to the world. It was very secret song, which I loved, and also I am a sucker for many florals. I bought them and wore them to my book launches in Vancouver and Toronto. If anybody is here for the bottomless well of '90s nostalgia, it's me.

But nostalgia has its limits, and I like interrogating things too much to truly pine for the past. Challenging myths, recontextualizing stories, reappraising what we think we knew, and identifying whose voices/perspectives are missing, erased, or purposefully excluded — this is what's been driving my writing for a long time, and it's also the crux of so much of the media and pop culture driving the ongoing '90s revival. From podcasts like *You're Wrong About* and *You Must Remember This* to first-person essays and in-depth reported features to bio-docs and memoirs, we're in a golden age of course correction and setting the record straight, drawing direct connections between the good and bad and in-between of the past and present. The '90s, as it pertains to music, means third-wave feminism, empowerment, and women leading record sales en masse for the first time. It also means sexism, misogyny, racism, transphobia, homophobia, and white feminism. Identifying the harm, naming the systems of oppression, and unpacking the truth — it's a massive reckoning and the '90s has as much to apologize and be held accountable for as it does to celebrate.

Dion, Twain, Morissette, and McLachlan experienced an onslaught of viciously gendered criticism, sexism, and misogyny, and they weren't alone. In 1992, Sinéad O'Connor was on the verge of pop stardom. Instead, she ended up a pariah for a number of years and subject to intense vitriol and violence after she tore up a picture of Pope John Paul II on *Saturday Night Live* and said "fight the real enemy" in protest of the Catholic Church's complicity in child sexual abuse. The blowback was massive, O'Connor was vilified, and her career never recovered. Not even when, nine years later, the Pope finally acknowledged sexual abuse within the Church. O'Connor was right, but the damage was done.

In her 2021 book, *Rememberings*, O'Connor wrote that she had zero regrets about tearing up that photo. "Everyone wants a pop star, see? But I am a protest singer. I just had stuff to get off my chest. I had no desire for fame. Having a No. 1 record derailed my career, and my tearing the photo put me back on the right track.”[1] She was also interviewed for the 2022 documentary *Nothing Compares*, which chronicled O’Connor’s rise and fall from 1987 to 1993. Upon its release, critics praised the film’s feminist lens and for finally giving O’Connor her due. *Nothing Compares* literally makes space for the singer-songwriter to tell her own story in her own words, functioning as the film’s narrator, and it’s as raw and real as O’Connor herself. “There was no therapy when I was growing up, so that’s the reason I got into music,” O’Connor explains at one point. “It was therapy. This is why it was such a shock to become a pop star. It was not what I wanted. I just wanted to scream.”[2]

O’Connor died on July 26, 2023, but her scream echoes on in her songs. Her sudden passing at just fifty-six years old triggered a flood of hindsight praise and an outpouring of reflections with headlines like “Sinéad O’Connor Was Right All Along,” “Sinéad O’Connor Redefined Pop Stardom. It Came at a Cost,” and “Remembering Sinéad O’Connor’s Sublime Music and Righteous Rage.” Hanif Abdurraqib’s brilliant *New Yorker* essay “Sinéad O’Connor Was Always Herself” opens with this line: “The Irish musician Sinéad O’Connor died, on Wednesday, at the age of fifty-six, without having received adequate apologies from this society we inhabit, which is often fuelled by an obsession with doling out gleeful, prolonged punishment.” Abdurraqib details the myriad ways in which O’Connor was dehumanized publicly over and over, but he also makes space for the ways in which she reasserted her humanity and heart in her music and through her

1 Ashley King, “Sinéad O’Connor’s Controversies — What Happened in the ’90s?” *Digital Music News*, July 31, 2023, https://www.digitalmusicnews.com/2023/07/31/sinead-o-connor-controversies-in-the-90s/.

2 *Nothing Compares*, directed by Kathryn Ferguson, 2022.

activism. "In an interview in 2021, O'Connor said that she liked solitude," Abdurraqib writes. "But the world owed her more than it gave, and so maybe she withdrew from it. Withdrawing is one way of managing expectations."[3]

O'Connor should be alive, and I don't know why she's not. The coroner's report indicated that she died of natural causes, but the amount of hate, ridicule, and scorn that she endured in her lifetime was unnatural, inexcusable, and unforgiveable. There was so much money made at her expense and there was real harm done to her as a result. O'Connor's story of gross mistreatment in the public eye is one familiar to many famous "problematic" women. At the other end of the '90s was Britney Spears who became a blockbuster pop star at eighteen years old with her 1999 debut, . . . *Baby One More Time*. An overnight tabloid sensation, Spears also became the face of numerous debates about the validity of pop music as an art form, sexualizing teenaged girls and whether they could or did have agency, and, essentially, whether teen pop musicians were even artists or just studio concoctions. Spears's exploitation continued throughout the 2000s, and she was a frequent target of the paparazzi documenting seemingly erratic public meltdowns that included her shaving her head, which O'Connor had also done almost two decades earlier when her record label attempted to control her appearance.

Spears's situation was further complicated in 2008 when a judge placed her under a conservatorship overseen by her father, Jamie Spears. A #FreeBritney campaign by fans began to champion Spears's autonomy, and in 2021, she successfully argued to

3 Hanif Abdurraqib, "Sinéad O'Connor Was Always Herself," *New Yorker*, July 29, 2023, https://www.newyorker.com/culture/listening-booth/sinead-oconnor-was-always-herself.

resume legal control of her life. Spears posted a lengthy audio clip on Twitter (which she later deleted) detailing her life under almost fourteen years of conservatorship. "It was all premeditated. A woman introduced the idea to my dad, and my mom actually helped him follow through and made it all happen," Spears said, according to a *Buzzfeed* article that excerpted quotes from Spears's audio clip. "It was all basically set up. There was no drugs in my system, no alcohol, nothing — it was pure abuse."[4]

Spears described years of control and verbal, emotional, and financial abuse. She wasn't allowed to have friends, choose her children's nannies, or have her own money, and was hospitalized against her will when she finally started to stand up for herself. But she was expected to work. "I was just like a robot, honestly. I didn't give a fuck anymore because I couldn't go where I wanted to go. It was just demoralizing. I was kind of like in this conspiracy thing of people claiming and treating me like a superstar, but yet they treated me like nothing." Spears's memoir is titled *The Woman in Me* — which is also the title of Twain's album and song — borrows from Spears's own song "Not a Girl (Not Yet a Woman) and was released on October 24, 2023, and became an instant bestseller. Before its publication, rumours ran amok that at least two of her famous exes had panicked and consulted lawyers to try to mitigate any potential fallout. Spears's liberation made a variety of cisgender men very nervous, and *The Woman in Me* delivered on its hype. I'm glad her book buried them all — especially Justin Timberlake, who allegedly pushed her to have

4 Stephanie K. Baer, "Britney Spears Said Her Conservatorship Was a Huge Setup in a 22-Minute Audio Recording Detailing What Happened to Her," *Buzzfeed*, August 29, 2022, https://www.buzzfeednews.com/article/skbaer/britney-spears-conservatorship-set-up-audio-recording.

an abortion and then dumped her via text — but most of all, I hope that in reclaiming her voice she finally feels some agency over her own life and can start to heal.

There's a dispiriting reality surrounding many superstar women who've ultimately had little control over their own stories, their music and art, their depictions in the media, their mental health and well-being, and their money. They're treated as puppets or ghosts, robots and commodities, props that are expected to perform, entertain, and decorate the world. The sexism and misogyny are rampant, and when racism factors in, the violence escalates and so does the erasure. Pop/R&B trio TLC (Tionne "T-Boz" Watkins, Rozonda "Chilli" Thomas, and the late Lisa "Left Eye" Lopes, who died in 2002) is the best-selling girl group of all time (85 million records sold worldwide as of May 2023[5]), and they dominated the 1990s: TLC's 1992 album, *Ooooooohhh . . . On the TLC Tip*, sold more than four million copies in the USA; 1994's follow-up, *CrazySexyCool*, sold more than fourteen million copies; and the third record, 1999's *FanMail*, sold more than ten million records and yet they still didn't (and don't) get the respect or attention they deserved (and deserve) from mainstream media outlets.

At *Variety*'s 2023 Power of Women luncheon, TLC received the Legacy Award, and in her speech, Chilli opened up about some of the discrimination the band faced at the height of their fame. "When you are a woman of color, it's real hard — it's a huge struggle. I'll always remember when 'No Scrubs' came out and it was actually our first number one . . . I always wanted

5 Jason Lamphier, "TLC on Their New Documentary and Why 'No Scrubs' Would Be 'Bumping on the Radio' if It Came Out Today," *Entertainment Weekly*, May 11, 2023, https://ew.com/music/tlc-forever-documentary-hot-summer-nights-tour-interview/.

to be on the cover of *Rolling Stone* magazine . . . we didn't get the cover. I won't say who [got the cover], it's okay because he deserved it, too, but we also did. The message was 'the last time we had someone Black on the cover, it didn't really sell well.'"[6] Conversely, Morissette (1995 and 1998), Twain (1998), and McLachlan (1998) all received *Rolling Stone* covers at the heights of their sales successes. Jar Jar Binks, Beavis and Butt-Head, and Bart Simpson all received *RS* covers in the 1990s. The *Seinfeld* cast was featured twice. Gender representation on *RS* covers in the '90s is terrible, but the overwhelming whiteness is egregious. Most years, at least two Black artists or groups appeared on *RS* covers, but 1991 dedicated just a part of a cover to a Black act (De La Soul was part of a composite cover with several other acts), and 1994 featured just one Black artist on its cover: the late Bob Marley. Justice for TLC!

There was some American music industry infrastructure and support for Black artists making soul, R&B, and hip hop in the '90s. The same could not be said for Canada. Canada's music industry was always whitewashed, and Black artists either struggled to fit in, felt their Blackness was being erased, or had to leave the country to make it big. Deborah Cox is now known as the "Queen of R&B" and she's credited with putting R&B on the Canadian map, but when she first started out looking for a record label in the '90s, every major Canadian outfit turned her down. Cox had no choice but to try her luck in Los Angeles. In 1994, Clive Davis heard her demo and signed Cox to a record deal. She was twenty-one years old when her self-titled

---

6 Thania Garcia, "TLC's Chilli Remembers Losing Out on Magazine Covers Over the Claim That Black Artists 'Didn't Really Sell Well,'" *Variety*, April 4, 2023, https://variety.com/2023/music/news/tlc-chilli-magazine-covers-black-artists-1235573365/.

debut was released, and though it wasn't a blockbuster success, it hit #1 on the Billboard Heatseekers chart and launched Cox into the spotlight. "All that struggle and challenge led up to the outpouring of the style of songs in that first album, because it just had to be bulletproof," Cox told me for a 2020 CBC Music interview. "There was a bit of pressure for it to work and for it to be successful. As soon as you heard the music, you would know that there was something different, something special and something unique about this situation. And I think that's what we were really striving for: I didn't want to be like everybody else."

Cox wasn't like everyone else, and she reaffirmed that with her 1998 follow-up, *One Wish*, which went platinum. That pressure to make something "bulletproof" was also part of the burden of representation. Cox was considered Canada's first Black woman R&B/pop/soul superstar. Her success could open doors for other young Black artists coming up behind her, but only if she was among the best. She also didn't have any peers with whom she could share this part of her journey.

> There's a lot of loneliness. I think there's a lot of unsurety, too, because as a pioneer, you just don't know the inroads you're making. You don't know how far you're actually going and there's no one there to cheer you on really outside of your own bubble. You don't really have any perspective, you just know what it's like when it's done and it's decades later and people remember . . . Being a pioneer has its pros and cons, I guess. More pros outweigh the cons at the end of the day, because

> you essentially are noted for your uniqueness and for being the first.[7]

But that acknowledgement isn’t always guaranteed, and if it does arrive, it can take decades. Cox has had a great career, and she is talented enough to have diversified, breaking out on Broadway and as a film and television actor. She has won four Juno Awards so far, and in 2022 she was inducted in the Canadian Music Hall of Fame, where she made history yet again as the first Black woman inductee in its history. In 2022. Over the last decade, Drake and the Weeknd, both Black male artists, have become global superstars, but Black Canadian women musicians have yet to break out in the same way.

Jessie Reyez, a pop/R&B singer-songwriter who is Colombian Canadian, has been holding the industry and her label to account since her breakthrough debut, 2017’s *Kiddo*. On the song “Gatekeeper,” Reyez blasted the sexism and sexual misconduct she’d experienced as a young woman, eviscerating the then-unnamed man who abused her and threatened to derail her career. In 2020, Reyez protested loudly and publicly in solidarity with the Black community against anti-Black racism, and she encouraged fellow Latinx performers to join her. She also participated in a special CTV newscast called *Change & Action: Racism in Canada* during which she shared a series of bleak statistics about

7 Andrea Warner, “Will Canada Ever Deserve Deborah Cox?” CBC Music, September 10, 2020, https://www.cbc.ca/music/will-canada-ever-deserve-deborah-cox-1.5714490.

racial inequality at Canada's three major record labels. She then called on the executives directly and by name: "I want to implore Shane Carter from Sony Music Canada, I want to implore Jeffrey Remedios at Universal Music Canada, who I know personally, and Steve Kane at Warner Music Canada: If you guys are hearing this, or watching this, you guys have the power right now in your hands to be pioneers and to be legitimate allies."[8]

Reyez is among a vibrant generation of young artists and activists who are quick to call out inequality and inequity and interested in genuine accountability, inclusiveness, and restorative justice. She's also one of many who cites Morissette as an influence. In 2022, Reyez, Serena Ryder, and Alessia Cara all performed tributes to Morissette when she was inducted into the Canadian Songwriters Hall of Fame (CSHP). Reyez, who offered up a powerhouse performance of "Ironic," was nervous to sing in front of one of her idols. She was also anxious about the song's "hella fast" register switch, Reyez told *The Mancurian*, but her manager reassured Reyez that even if she did mess up, Alanis would love it because she is, after all, "the queen of imperfections." Reyez made sure to give Morissette her flowers while she had the chance. "I let her know that she made me feel at home in my mistakes, which is a gift for anybody but from [a] Canadian woman to another Canadian woman, it just feels a little more intimate."[9]

Grammy Award–winning singer-songwriter Olivia Rodrigo was also on hand to induct Morissette into the CSHF. Rodrigo

---

8 CTV. *Change & Action: Racism in Canada*, aired June 13, 2020.

9 Jay Darcy, "YESSIE: In Conversation with Jessie Reyez," *Mancunion*, January 23, 2023, https://mancunion.com/2023/01/23/yessie-in-conversation-with-jessie-reyez/.

isn't Canadian, but as soon as her breakthrough hit single, "drivers license," was released in January 2021, the eighteen-year-old's broken-hearted and enraged anthem had me feeling that same gut punch and visceral thrill of hearing Morissette's "You Oughta Know" for the first time. When Rodrigo's debut album, *Sour*, was finally released four months later, it was a spiritual and sonic successor to *Jagged Little Pill* and a clear indicator that the '90s revival wasn't going away. I wasn't the only one who clocked the relationship between the two records. In October 2021, *Rolling Stone* brought the singer-songwriters together for a photoshoot and conversation. It was their first meeting and the beginning of a fast friendship. Rodrigo brought Morissette on stage at her L.A. concert in early 2022 where they performed "You Oughta Know." Months later, Rodrigo gave a personal and heartwarming speech at Morissette's induction into the CSHF.

> I was thirteen when I first heard *Jagged Little Pill*, and my life was completely changed. Alanis's songwriting was unlike anything I had ever heard before, and I haven't heard anything quite like it since. And that voice — fierce and tender and sometimes funny and playful. I became hooked for life. Alanis captures the anger, the grief, and the love of the human experience better than anyone. Her songs unite people, empower people, and help them heal. Alanis, you are a trailblazer, and you have inspired an entire generation of uncompromising, radically honest songwriting — but even more than your long list of musical achievements, I look up to your character and your kindness most

> of all. . . . I'll carry the advice that you've given me my whole life, and if they had a Hall of Fame for being the most incredible human being, with the biggest heart, I'm a hundred percent positive you'd be inducted into that one as well.[10]

Honestly, more of this, please. I love to see the intergenerational relationships between artists and records, how the music that "made" them shows up in their own albums. But I would also love to see more acknowledgement of Canada's long history of whitewashing its music industry and what its powerholders are doing now to change it. I'd love to hear more from the racialized, queer, and gender nonconforming fans from the '90s who contributed to the success of Dion, Twain, Morissette, and McLachlan.

In 2021, Candice Frederick wrote an incredible piece for the *Huffington Post* called "The 'Jagged' Documentary Doesn't Feature Any Women of Color. That Is a Huge Misstep." Frederick, a Black woman, opens by referencing Morissette's 1995 *Rolling Stone* cover labelling her an "Angry White Female" and contextualizes the factors: Morissette was twenty-one and on the cover of a magazine owned by white men that typically featured other white men in that pride of place. "In a sense, the moniker was a backhanded compliment," Frederick writes. But "the aforementioned title applied to Morissette has a similar effect as the Angry Black Woman label that is in equal parts affirming and reductive. And there's not a single Black or brown woman interviewed in the film who might have pointed this out."

---

10 Canadian Songwriters Hall of Fame, "Olivia Rodrigo Inducts Alanis Morissette into the Canadian Songwriters Hall of Fame," YouTube, https://www.youtube.com/watch?v=GrM5V0Z1owc.

Jagged is missing essential voices and perspectives, Frederick states, pointing out that “*Jagged Little Pill* unapologetically articulated the rage young women of color have but are too often advised to suppress — and Morissette was ultimately well-rewarded for it.” Frederick interviews two women who were fans of the album growing up — Cari Garcia, a Latina food blogger and therapist, and Colleen Armstrong, a Black independent media consultant — who share how deeply they related to *Jagged Little Pill* as young people. “Growing up in a Latin, Hispanic household, girls are scrutinized for pretty much everything,” Garcia told Frederick. “For the first time, it was an album that got me. [Morissette’s] cultural identity — that’s not something I was thinking at fourteen. I felt so lost and in a lot of pain.”

For Armstrong, *JLP* modelled a different way to be in the world, a hidden “other side” of her that had yet to reveal itself. Frederick explains that “part of the reason why Armstrong felt the need to control that side of her was because of the way Black and brown women’s emotions were policed in the ’90s.” Armstrong has changed since then, Frederick writes, even though the rest of the world hasn’t come very far. For fans like Garcia and Armstrong, “whose feelings were stifled in the ’90s and omitted from *Jagged*,” Frederick points to Frankie Healy, one of the main characters in the Broadway musical *Jagged Little Pill*. The character is a Black bisexual teenaged girl who is being raised by her adoptive white family. Morgan Dudley, the actor playing Frankie at the time, tells Frederick about relating to the experience of being a Black person raised by a white family and the difficult conversations she left unsaid for a long time. When Dudley did finally open up, it ultimately helped her own family grow closer. “I feel like this musical is giving people the space to be honest with themselves, to be honest in their experiences and feel safe to have the emotions that they might have about that," Dudley tells Frederick. "It's very validating, I think."[11]

These perspectives would have added so much to *Jagged*, and Frederick's work here is essential. She shouldn't have been one of the only writers to point this out or write a brilliant piece about it. Twain's documentary would also have benefitted from more racialized voices (Lionel Richie makes an appearance), especially Black and Indigenous women's voices who could also speak to the ways in which racialized women are treated in country music and the ways racialized women's bodies are policed, scrutinized, and overly sexualized (usually to their detriment) in society at large and in country music. And to also address Twain's claims to Indigenous identity and how misleading claims like hers do real damage to Indigenous artists who are grossly underrepresented. Mickey Guyton and Crystal Shawanda might have been excellent additions to *Not Just a Girl*.

This ongoing '90s revival isn't just about nostalgia; to be truly effective, it needs to be more inclusive and meaningfully diverse, especially when it comes to Dion, Twain, Morissette, and McLachlan. Racialized people are an important and substantial part of the fan bases for global superstars. At best, these fans have rarely been properly acknowledged; at worst, they've been erased. If, as a society, we're going to reclaim the narratives of maligned, misunderstood, and mistreated '90s superstars, we

11 Candice Frederick, "The 'Jagged' Documentary Doesn't Feature Any Women of Color. That Is a Huge Misstep," *Huffington Post*, November 26, 2021, https://www.huffpost.com/entry/jagged-documentary-alanis-morissette-hbo_n_619d173ce4b044a1cc0d6c96.

can't keep whitewashing the experts, talking heads, and cultural commentators.

I think the ongoing obsession with the '90s is also about a desire to figure out how that decade and its supposed liberalness can be used to understand the current social schism of very loud, rich, far-right conservatives and wannabe fascists versus a genuinely progressive groundswell of young activists who are pushing back against racism, transphobia, homophobia, climate injustice, labour exploitation, and other inequities. As a former teenaged girl in the '90s, I can see now that the decade was rife with as many places of refuge as danger zones, a *supposed* liberalness that I wasn't able to acknowledge because I was so steeped in my own internalized misogyny. That conflict can be a mirror, perhaps, for the sociopolitical divisions of today, and maybe something can be gleaned from the art creators made then for the creators making art now.

The last ten years have continued to deepen my appreciation for Dion and Twain, and I keep discovering deeper commonalities in the themes of all four artists whose global domination soundtracked my formative years. I learned to stand up for myself and fight in the fury, wit, and unapologetic mess of Morissette's songs. I figured out ways to grieve and recognize beauty in McLachlan's songs. When I finally accepted Twain's invitation to go with the girls, I unlocked a kind of pleasure I'd previously been denying myself. Credit to all of these women, but most of all Dion, for helping me embrace the full spectrum of my emotions and realizing angst isn't more real than earlier hopefulness. And these women are not past tense; they are firmly present and continuing to evolve, some even participating in their own '90s revival and reckoning. If there's one legacy that all four artists share, it's that they offered up their own versions of radical honesty. This is what younger musicians like Jessie Reyez and Olivia Rodrigo are responding to, because truth is timeless and it's liberating. Dion, Twain, Morissette, and McLachlan carved out space for themselves and kicked open doors for other women, and they weren't perfect. They were messy and complicated and had to figure out being so very human in public.

Love them or hate them, they were (and are) always themselves, and that is how they became the best-selling Canadian artists in Canada and influenced generations of people to unapologetically embrace every failure and every feeling. It might have taken me a couple of decades to fully appreciate the Venn diagram of Dion, Twain, Morissette, and McLachlan, but I see it now so clearly. They spoke up and sang out and held nothing back, and people wanted to hear what they had to say. Between 1993 and 1997, they showed me a kind of power and possibility that I didn't yet know was unique. They normalized women's voices taking up space at a time when I didn't understand that this ubiquity was unprecedented. Dion, Twain, Morissette, and McLachlan laid a foundation for me and countless others in ways that I am still figuring out and unpacking today and probably for decades to come. Teenaged me still can't quite believe it, but it turns out that Dion, Morissette, Twain, and McLachlan are my fab four. Bigger than the Beatles. That doesn't just sound right; it feels right.

ACKNOWLEDGEMENTS

It's such a pleasure to revisit this book, adding to it and strengthening it almost a decade after its first release. Thank you so much to Jen Sookfong Lee and the ECW team for seeing *We Oughta Know*'s potential and championing it (and me). It means the world to me. Also, working with Jen continues to be one of the greatest pleasures of my life. She is the best and I will fight for her forever and always (not that she needs me to, but if she does, I'm there).

Thank you also to all of the other wonderful ECW folks, especially Jen Knoch, Jessica Albert, Victoria Cozza, Emily Varsava, Emily Ferko, Cassie Smyth, and Crissy Boylan.

Thank you, Eternal Cavalier Press for reaching out in 2014 and asking if I had any ideas for a book. I appreciate you taking a chance on me and supporting the first version of *We Oughta Know*.

Thank you, Carlos Hernandez Fisher, Cynara Geissler, Holly Gordon, and Jackie Wong for reading early drafts of this book, both in 2014 and in 2023, and providing such careful, thoughtful, and generous feedback. I love you all and trust you implicitly. I'm so lucky to have you in my life.

Thank you, Vivek Shraya for writing a magnificent foreword for this book and for being such a fierce supporter of my writing. It means so much to me that a brilliant artist like you sees me the way that you do.

Thank you to my agent, Carolyn Forde, who said yes to a cold-call coffee invitation and has been making my life better ever since. Thank you to my colleagues at CBC Music for making me a better writer and thinker, and to all of the editors I've worked with over the years.

Thank you to my family, friends, and loved ones past and present who have been with me throughout the journey of this book. Carlos, you are my heart. I love you. I want to especially thank my sister, Jenn, my mom, Elsie, and my paternal grandmother, Lena. You love and support me no matter what, and that means more to me than you know. You didn't ask for me to be a writer and you didn't ask to show up in my books, and it isn't always easy. I want to acknowledge that.

Thank you to Céline Dion, Shania Twain, Alanis Morissette, and Sarah McLachlan for sharing your music and yourselves with the world for so long. I don't know if the trade was worth it for all of you, but your existence and your music have literally changed my life. I am endlessly grateful for the ways in which I was able to figure out aspects of myself through my parasocial relationships to you.

And to everyone who read *We Oughta Know* in its first incarnation: thank you! Many of you have reached out to me over the years and I love hearing from you. It's a wild thing to publish your first book and then find out it means something special to other people you don't even know! I hope you all enjoy this expanded, enriched *We Oughta Know* as much as I enjoyed digging back into it again all these years later. Nineties vibes forever, patriarchy never.

Portions of "Making Peace with Céline Dion" and "Shania Twain" reprinted courtesy of CBC Music.

APPENDIX

'90s Forever — A Compendium of Awesome Canadian Women Musicians

I've always loved lists. I was a weird kid, and one of my favourite things to do when I was thirteen was write and rewrite lists of all my Sweet Valley High books and Baby-Sitters Club books. I practised my handwriting, it made me feel orderly, and it was a useful system of cataloguing serials, which is why I'm falling back on it with this alphabetized primer of the Canadian '90s acts (solo women or women-fronted bands) that everybody needs to know.

Alannah Myles, 1989–present
Toronto, ON
Key '90s songs: "Black Velvet," "Song Instead of a Kiss"

The "Black Velvet" singer never quite recaptured the lightning in a bottle of her smash debut, but Myles's presence still loomed large over the early part of the '90s. Her image and voice recalled a fusion of Joan Jett and Heart, personifying a sexy sort of danger. Her womanliness — that brilliant shock of grey hair falling down the side of her face in the video for "Song Instead of a

Kiss" — was actually celebrated by the very industry known for glorifying, exploiting, and prioritizing youthful allure.

Amanda Marshall, 1995–present
Toronto, ON
Key '90s songs: "Birmingham," "Dark Horse," "Let It Rain"

From the outset, Marshall was conflated with Morissette and then eclipsed entirely, and this is nonsense for a variety of reasons, the most important being that they sound nothing alike, vocally or musically. But both had long curtains of hair and both were women vocalists, so, you know, basically the same, right? Nope. Marshall's songs didn't have the same urgency as Morissette's, nor did she write all of her own material, but they resonated. She tackled common themes of love and heartache, but she also touched on class, domestic violence, racism, and identity politics (Marshall is a Black woman, born to a Black father and a white mother), and her voice is among the most distinctive Canada's ever known.

Bif Naked, 1994–present
Vancouver, BC
Key '90s songs: "Daddy's Getting Married," "Tell on You (Letter to My Rapist)," "Lucky," "Chotee"

Full disclosure: I love Bif. In 2001, after journalism school, I started a magazine, *Medusa*, with a group of friends and classmates. We were an alt-women's magazine and pansexual, dealing with entertainment, arts, culture, sex, and politics. We fancied ourselves subversive types, and I think we even succeeded in a few ways. Bif was the cover model for our debut issue and also for our fifth and final issue two years later. I loved her music, the signature inky-black eyeliner, her tattoos, her honesty, just everything about her. And she was kind; she *is* kind. Bif wrote frank, heartfelt, punk-as-fuck songs about rape, abortion, love, and heartbreak. She refused to make things cleaner or neater or sanitized. She kept showing the world there were different types of girls. In doing so, she showed girls there were different ways to live, there was a place for women in punk rock, and she embodied the importance of being true to yourself, no apologies.

Chantal Kreviazuk, 1996–present
Winnipeg, MB
Key '90s songs: "Surrounded," "God Made Me"

Kreviazuk's voice has personality, a rough beauty, and the way it crashed up and against her piano, each pushing the other to new heights — it was a sound that was just different enough in 1997 to warrant its own spotlight. Kreviazuk also had a unique lyrical voice as a writer: the smidgens of religious imagery balanced with so many other facets of her personality — wry, funny, weird, frustrated, unapologetic.

cub, 1992–1997
Vancouver, BC
Key '90s songs: "Magic 8 Ball," "New York City," "Freaky"

Whether you consider cub cuddlecore or pop-punk depends on whether you're in on the joke or whether you find the former term kind of sexist. Regardless, cub became synonymous with cuddlecore after a friend of the band jokingly described their sound as such, and cub ran with it. Initially, anyway. The Vancouver-based band (originally Lisa Marr, Robynn Iwata, and Valeria Fellini until 1994, when Lisa G. replaced Fellini) made sunny-sounding punk that rode the switchblade's edge between twee and aggressive. The band also featured a few appearances by a then-unknown Neko Case, who was inspired to start her own group, Maow, a few years later.

Dayna Manning, 1997–present
Stratford, ON / Calgary, AB
Key '90s song: "Half the Man"

Manning was barely eighteen when she released her debut album, but the sound was that of a woman wise beyond her years who also possessed a distinct singing style. Her first single, the darkly beautiful "Half the Man," is a mournful little folk song and possesses all the hallmarks of an instant classic. It has a hypnotic, haunted, Maritime vibe, as if Manning were a pirate in a previous life and this was an old shanty lost to the sea until 1997.

Deborah Cox, 1995–present
Toronto, ON
Key '90s songs: "Nobody's Supposed to Be Here," "Things Just Ain't the Same"

We really screwed up in not appreciating Deborah Cox in the '90s when we should have, but there's still time to right this wrong. The R&B vocalist's range, style, and attitude were somewhat wasted on most of Canada, unfortunately. Even now, our country has an overabundance of successful white musicians considering the diversity of our population — and yes, I say that in full acknowledgement of the fact that this is a book about how four white women became Canada's best-selling artists. I can't change that aspect of the story, nor can I retroactively give Cox the superstar career she deserves. She got pigeonholed as the face of diversity, treated more as a novelty than the substantial artist that she is, and that's on us, Canada. Cox, however, is living her best life. She's as busy as ever, having branched out into acting in TV and film, as well as starring on Broadway, and, of course, still touring. She's booked, busy, and killing it.

Diana Krall, 1990–present
Nanaimo, BC
Key '90s songs: "Boulevard of Broken Dreams," "All or Nothing at All"

Krall's jazz standards seemed to exist on another plane compared to the music most often associated with Canadian women artists in the '90s, but her output was steady and strong throughout the decade. She released five albums in seven years, many of which enjoyed massive chart success, even before her huge pop crossover in the 2000s. This entire book was inspired by the fact that Dion, Twain, Morissette, and McLachlan are the four best-selling Canadian artists. The next best-selling Canadian artist? Diana Krall.

Esthero, 1997–present
Toronto, ON
Key '90s songs: "Heaven Sent," "That Girl"

Jenny-Bea Englishman, a.k.a. Esthero, is a singer-songwriter whose trip-hop debut was a modest success in Canada. Its sole single, "Heaven Sent," helped launch her internationally, which secured future collaborations with a variety of high-profile pop and rap acts.

Emm Gryner, 1995–present
Toronto, ON
Key '90s song: "Summerlong"

To describe Gryner as a prolific songwriter barely does her justice. Between 1995 and 1999, she released four records — and that was just the beginning. Her pop songs didn't necessarily translate into huge hits, save for "Summerlong," but they are well-crafted gems and garnered her big-name fans in the songwriting community. And from the outset, Gryner displayed a savvy wisdom when it came to her career, starting her own label with her debut record and enjoying high-profile collaborations with the likes of David Bowie and Def Leppard.

Feist, 1999–present
Toronto, ON
Key '90s songs: "Monarch," "Cool to Love Your Family"

Leslie Feist emerged from the punk scene in Calgary and relocated to Toronto, where she released 1999's *Monarch (Lay Your Jewelled Head Down)*. It's a strong first record, and the clarity of Feist's vision is evident from the very first track, but it wasn't a hit. In fact, Feist wouldn't become a household name until five years later. But spend a little time with *Monarch* and marvel at how unobscured her vocals are. The layers of sound and the precise architecture of her future material is great, but there's also something wonderful about hearing Feist let her voice soar up and above the instrumentation.

Holly Cole, 1983–present
Halifax, NS / Toronto, ON
Key '90s songs: "Onion Girl," "Make It Go Away"

Cole's jazz trio experimented with pop and rock songs from the very beginning, but they had an even more eclectic side that shone through with their 1995 album of Tom Waits covers, *Temptation*. The big pop crossover came on 1997's *Dark Dear Heart*, which catapulted Cole out of the nightclubs and onto the top 40 stations and MuchMusic rotation.

Holly McNarland, 1995–present
Winnipeg, MB
Key '90s songs: "Numb," "Coward"

Alongside Morissette, Kim Stockwood, and at times McLachlan, McNarland is also considered an "angry woman," which was aggravating and myopic and wrong, of course. McNarland possessed a fragile ferocity as she gripped her guitar and attacked her lyrics. It felt like the walls were coming down on our own private hells, like there were others like us who felt distraught, disaffected, depressed, unsure of the world. A community was fostered in that shared frustration. Her quiet frankness in "Coward" is another revelatory moment, thanks to the heartbreakingly typical way she enumerates, over and over again, her seemingly endless "faults," all of which are like a laundry list of every negative thought a woman in an abusive relationship has ever had about herself. It is deeply, distressingly relatable to this day.

Jale, 1992–1996
Halifax, NS
Key '90s songs: "Not Happy," "Double Edge"

Jale (Jennifer Pierce, Alyson MacLeod, Laura Stein, and Eve Hartling), the scrappy grunge-turned-power-pop group, was short on actual lifespan, but their legend looms large even now. They're credited with co-founding Halifax's grunge / punk / indie scene and the Halifax pop explosion alongside peers like Sloan, the Super Friendz, and Eric's Trip. Jale signed to Seattle's famed Sub Pop label, home to Nirvana, Mudhoney, and the flourishing grunge scene. Jale was the second of several Canadian bands that Sub Pop ultimately signed, solidifying Halifax's reputation as the place to be for music in the early '90s. Jale was also something of a rarity at the time, given that the band was composed entirely of women (until MacLeod left in 1995), and this catapulted them into a different spotlight, too, as Canada's unofficial answer to the Riot Grrrl movement.

Jann Arden, 1993–present
Calgary, AB
Key '90s songs: "Insensitive," "I Would Die for You," "Unloved"

Listening to Arden's first two albums felt like she'd opened up her heart and invited all of us inside, unconcerned with preserving herself or her dignity, unashamed of her insecurities or desires. It was hugely freeing to listen to her admit her fears and see her draw strength from vulnerability, rather than it weakening her. On paper, Arden's debut single, "I Would Die for You," is as fatalistic as a Céline Dion forever love song, yet Arden's delivery emphasizes that the sentiment is a painful, problematic one, not romantic. But it is songs like "Insensitive," "Unloved," and "Good Mother" that prove how adept she was (and is) at navigating the nuances of life's biggest hurts.

Julie Doiron / Broken Girl, 1996–present
Halifax, NS
Key '90s songs: "Soon, Coming Closer," "Love to Annoy"

Shortly before Doiron's band, Eric's Trip, broke up, she released her debut solo album as Broken Girl. It's a lo-fi heartbreaker inspired by her own breakup with Eric's Trip bandmate Rick White, hence the devastatingly accurate name she recorded under. Once that first post-breakup album was out of her system, Doiron decided to record under her own name, and it's no exaggeration to say everything she's ever done is exquisite. Her '90s solo material is unlike anything else recorded in the country, even though at its most surface level it is, yes, another girl with a guitar. But Doiron's songs are tiny wings, graceful and strong despite the veneer of fragility.

Kim Stockwood, 1995–present
St. John's, NL / Toronto, ON
Key '90s songs: "Jerk," "She's Not in Love," "Enough Love"

You know what's better than a breakup song? A fuck-you breakup song, particularly when the chorus is as satisfactorily repetitive as

"You jerk." Stockwood's kiss-off anthem is almost a schoolyard taunt, and yet it's an empowering piece of pop that inspired a cool sort of solidarity every time it came on the radio. Everyone has a jerk, right? In fact, her entire first album, *Bonavista*, felt like a triumph of sorts, an anti-love-song record that prioritized a woman's sense of self above all else. Thirty years later, I still think "Enough Love" should be mandatory listening for everyone.

Kinnie Starr, 1995–present
Calgary, AB / Vancouver, BC
Key '90s song: "Ophelia"

There was nobody more confounding or exciting in the '90s than Kinnie Starr. Blending hip hop, R&B, spoken word, alt-rock, and pop, Starr tackles topics like sex, Indigenous identity, social justice, feminism, sexism, equality, and women's rights. She took up space, took back space, and owned the multitudes she contained with inspiring confidence.

Loreena McKennitt, 1985–present
Stratford, ON
Key '90s song: "The Mummers' Dance"

McKennitt doesn't get the credit she deserves, which is something I realized when researching her for an interview a few years ago for CBC Music. She's been DIY since the beginning of her career, recording and releasing Celtic music via her own label, Quinlan Road. From the start, she built up a mailing list of loyal fans around the world, which afforded her the financial opportunity to make records herself without major label interference. A dance remix version of "The Mummers' Dance" gave McKennitt her first and only mainstream hit single in 1997, but it's the creative control and clarity of her vision that have made her one of the most quietly successful and inspirational people in Canadian music.

Mae Moore, 1985–present
Vancouver, BC
Key '90s songs: "Genuine," "Bohemia"

I had all but forgotten Moore, but once the spoken-word groove of her two most famous songs enter your brain, the thrill of recognition is like stumbling across a long-lost childhood friend. Moore's songs were somewhat lost in the shuffle of musician/woman/solo artist, that glorious Canadian trifecta (despite the fact that Our Lady Peace, Big Wreck, and countless other male alt-rock *Big Shiny Tunes* bands could thrive and survive at the same time). But Moore deserves to be remembered, particularly for the songs on which she fuses rock, pop, spoken word, and a little acid jazz for good measure.

Me Mom & Morgentaler / Mudgirl / The Kim Band, 1990–present
Montreal, QC / Vancouver, BC
Key '90s songs: "Oh Well," "What a Drag"

Kim Bingham cycled through a lot of band names and a lot of sounds, but it was that restless spirit that made her one of Canadian music's key innovators in the '90s. Me Mom & Morgentaler has a ska-inspired funk/rock vibe, Mudgirl experiments with guitar-driven pop, and the Kim Band coalesces garage-punk, pop melodies, and crunchy rock into a crashing tower of sound. Plus Bingham's command of guitar is like watching a cyclone turn a field: unrelenting, fierce, and totally awe-inspiring.

Mecca Normal, 1984–present
Vancouver, BC
Key '90s songs: "Vacant Night Sky," "Waiting for Rudy"

Underground art-punk-rock duo Jean Smith (vocalist) and David Lester (guitarist) have been crafting weird, tightly coiled but loosely structured songs about gender, feminism, politics, and social justice issues since 1984. Anybody who knows Beat Happening, Bikini Kill, and Sleater-Kinney should know Mecca Normal, but almost nobody does. I'm ashamed to admit that up until last year, I barely knew them, either. They're a hometown band and I'm a feminist who writes about music, and still I never came across Mecca Normal until someone alerted me to their existence after I wrote an essay about how much I missed the political fire of music from the '90s. Mecca Normal were Riot Grrrl and DIY before those movements existed, and they were tireless in their commitment to their art, releasing seven records in the '90s alone. In fact, Mecca Normal were basically doing the '90s in the '80s. Consider the still-relevant subject matter of their mid-'80s tunes like "Smile Baby," which calls out street harassment (yes, three decades ago), "More, More, More" and the privilege of white men and the American Dream, and affirming a woman's right to safety in a public space on the simple, chilling, and inspiring "I Walk Alone." It's important music that matters even more today.

Melanie Doane, 1993–present
Halifax, NS
Key '90s songs: "Adam's Rib," "Waiting for the Tide"

Doane's debut album is her best and most successful record to date, and it was a staple of my CD player in 1998. The title track, "Adam's Rib," is a brilliantly sarcastic feminist anthem written from the perspective of the rib that eventually goes on to make Eve (a very generous gesture, if controversially akin to cloning).

Maow, 1995–1996
Vancouver, BC
Key '90s songs: "Wank," "Ms. Lefevre"

Most famously, Maow is the short-lived pop-punk act that was co-fronted by Neko Case, but in their brief time together the trio (including Tobey Black and Corrina Beesley-Hammond) released an EP and a full-length album and, like cub, became something of an inspiration for other women and young girls to infiltrate the male-dominated punk rock scene.

Oh Susanna (a.k.a. Suzie Ungerleider), 1997–present
Vancouver, BC / Toronto, ON
Key '90s songs: "Shame," "Tangled & Wild"

Ungerleider's 1997 EP signalled the arrival of a distinct new talent in the folk-rock scene, and her voice as a writer and lyricist helped distinguish her as a no-fuss delight. On her 1999 debut album, *Johnstown*, she fully embraces alt-country, couching her stark, simple lyrical poetry in the two-armed embrace of a twangy guitar and lap steel. It's the perfect combination for her keenly observed, detail-rich songs, which absolutely vibrate with life.

Plumtree, 1993–2000
Halifax, NS
Key '90s songs: "Scott Pilgrim," "Go"

Plumtree's school of rock origins are the best: sisters Lynette and Carla Gillis (ages fourteen and sixteen, respectively) met Amanda Braden and Nina Martin (ages fifteen and sixteen) through their music teachers and formed a band. After Martin left two years later (and was replaced by Catriona Sturton), Plumtree had opened for a host of bands, including hometown neighbours Jale, had a full-length release to their credit, and amassed a small but strong following. The band's biggest claim to fame is the song "Scott Pilgrim," which inspired Canadian graphic novelist Bryan Lee O'Malley to borrow the name for the hero of his blockbuster six-part series (and its subsequent film adaptation, soundtrack, and video game).

Rebecca West, 1994–1996
Halifax, NS
Key '90s songs: "Sick," "Save It"

Rebecca West was a three-piece alt-rock/art-punk band, but the main draw was its charmingly wry singer-songwriter-guitarist, Allison Outhit. She was christened the "godmother of the Halifax scene" by no less than Sloan's Chris Murphy in *Have Not Been the Same: The CanRock Renaissance*. Outhit, previously of the rock band Bubaiskull, offered a helping hand in mentoring other young women new to Halifax's flourishing scene, as well as releasing two albums and an EP in the band's short but significant run.

Rose Chronicles, 1993–1996
Vancouver, BC
Key '90s songs: "Awaiting Eternity," "Dwelling"

Kristy Thirsk was the lead singer of this short-lived, dreamy art-pop band, and her vocals are really the shiny centrepiece of this affair. In fact, the band's debut full-length album, *Shiver*, had so much momentum it won the 1995 Juno Award for best alternative album. Their sound recalls the best aspects of acts like Sarah McLachlan and Tori Amos, but it doesn't make them inaccessible. If they hadn't broken up before the release of their second record, Rose Chronicles would likely be more than a footnote in Canada's alt-rock history.

Sarah Slean, 1997–present
Toronto, ON
Key '90s songs: "Playing Cards with Judas," "Blue Parade"

Inspired by cabaret music, Slean carved out a distinct niche for herself in the piano-driven, singer-songwriter '90s pop world. Her debut full-length record, *Blue Parade*, is a gorgeous, sombre affair that explores the hidden facets of darkness.

Susan Aglukark, 1992–present
Arviat, NU
Key '90s songs: "O Siem," "Hina Na Ho"

Aglukark is the first ever Inuk person to have a top 40 hit with "O Siem," which catapulted her to stardom across Canada. Her music infuses traditional Inuk sounds with pop, folk, and rock elements, crafting a sorely needed unique sonic landscape that remains accessible. Aglukark's success made her something of an ambassador for Indigenous artists in Canada in the '90s, and she's released seven more records since her 1995 breakthrough.

Tara MacLean, 1995–present
Charlottetown, PEI / Victoria, BC
Key '90s songs: "Evidence," "Let Her Feel the Rain"

It's not easy to take a song about child abuse, and the reckoning with truth that emerges out of silence, and make it catchy, beautiful, and chilling — but MacLean does it. Despite the dark subject matter, "Evidence" proved a powerful choice for her debut single: it was both a modest hit and established her as a voice capable of crafting good folk-pop out of tragic, terrible, but important subject matter.

Veda Hille, 1992–present
Vancouver, BC
Key '90s songs: "Small Weight," "Strange, Sad"

Hille is a poet, composer, lyricist, vocalist, pianist, and so much more. The inability to define her is probably both a blessing and a failure (on society's part, not hers). It kept Hille as something of a queen of the indies, widely respected and with plenty of freedom to follow her impulses into the wilder reaches of the dense forest that is her creative and brilliant brain. She never shies from a challenge, lyrically or musically; if anything, Hille's interest in daring herself or at least engaging with her curiosity, offered up delights ranging from piano-driven cabaret numbers to dark pop to avant-garde chamber rock. "Strange, Sad" is still perfection. Go listen to it now.

Weeping Tile, 1993–1998
Kingston, ON
Key '90s songs: "In the Road," "Through Yr Radio"

Sarah Harmer was the singer-songwriter for her alt-rock '90s band, and every track is a clear map leading towards the solo career that would explode at the start of the next decade. Weeping Tile has its own precision and beauty. The songs are richly textured and anchored in the depths of her vocals, rather than reaching up into the sky. The band's music explores themes of environmental distress, gender and feminism, mental health, and other politically charged issues with a high human cost.

Wild Strawberries, 1989–present
Toronto, ON
Key '90s songs: "Life Sized Marilyn Monroe," "Bet You Think I'm Lonely," "Crying Shame"

Comprised of married couple Roberta Harrison and Ken Harrison, Wild Strawberries is pure pop noir thanks to Roberta's distinctive vocals. It isn't just the husky, sexy, womanly nature of her delivery; there is something genuinely pleasing about the way she winds her tongue around the words that feels sophisticated and worldly. There are also provocative and political themes in their work, including sexism, feminism, poverty, and social justice. They basically seemed like the coolest couple ever: Roberta was the lead singer every girl wanted to be, and Ken was right there at her side. It was inspiring to young women, other musicians, fellow professionals (Roberta was also a physiotherapist and Ken a doctor), and young lovers that art, fame, creation, and equality could, for all appearances, go hand in hand.

CHLOE KRAUSE

Andrea Warner writes and talks. A lot. She is a settler who lives in Vancouver on the unceded territories of the Musqueam, Squamish, and Tsleil-Waututh First Nations. Her books include *The Time of My Life: Dirty Dancing*, *Rise Up and Sing! Power, Protest, and Activism in Music*, and *Buffy Sainte-Marie: The Authorized Biography*. Andrea is also an associate producer at CBC Music and the co-host of the weekly feminist pop culture podcast *Pop This!*